Credits

Author
Mark Aberdour

Reviewers
Anthony Borrow, S.J.

Silvina Paola Hillar

Ben Reynolds

Acquisition Editors
Vinay Argekar

Kunal Parikh

Lead Technical Editor
Neeshma Ramakrishnan

Technical Editors
Krutika Parab

Hardik B. Soni

Project Coordinator
Navu Dhillon

Proofreader
Dirk Manuel

Indexer
Tejal R. Soni

Production Coordinator
Aparna Bhagat

Cover Work
Aparna Bhagat

About the Author

Mark Aberdour is Head of Learning Platforms at UK learning technologies company, Epic. He has over 15 years of experience in software engineering, with professional roles in software testing, learning platforms development, and open source services delivery.

Mark has worked on over one hundred Moodle LMS and other learning technology implementation projects across a wide range of sectors, including healthcare, defense, retail, finance, engineering, automotive, higher and further education, and local and central government. Most of this has been with Epic, an industry leader in e-learning content, mobile learning solutions, and learning management systems implementation. Epic has led the way on mobile learning in workplace learning and development, hence Mark's focus on bringing mobile and Moodle together.

Mark was an early contributor to the original Bootstrap theme for Moodle and is credited as one of the founding team that built the Clean theme in Moodle 2.5, which is based on Bootstrap. Mark is a regular speaker at UK learning and development conferences, and presented at the UK and Ireland MoodleMoots in 2012 and 2013. He is also one of the founders of the MoodleBrighton user group, which meets monthly in Brighton, UK.

Moodle for Mobile Learning

Connect, communicate, and promote collaboration
with your coursework using Moodle

Mark Aberd

PUBLISI

BIRMINGHAM

Moodle for Mobile Learning

First published: September 2013

Production Reference: 1190913

Published by Packt Publishing Ltd.
Livery Place
35 Livery Street
Birmingham B3 2PB, UK.

ISBN 978-1-78216-438-8

www.packtpub.com

Cover Image by Suresh Mogre (suresh.mogre.99@gmail.com)

Acknowledgments

A huge debt of gratitude is owed to all of my colleagues at Epic. When I came back to the company in 2011, I had zero previous exposure to mobile learning, and the teams at Epic supported me on a huge learning curve with regards to what mobile learning is all about. With particular regards to this book, I would like to thank Imogen Casebourne and Ishmael Burdeau for initial ideas for content, and the wider Platforms and Mobile teams for their constant stream of inspiration and new ideas for what we can do with Moodle and mobile learning. I would also like to thank the project managers and sales and marketing team for chasing down permissions for the case studies.

I also owe thanks to a number of people for their assistance in writing this book:

Gavin Henrick for his sound advice on publishing a Moodle book based on the times he has done this himself.

Stuart Lamour, Carol Shergold, and Paulo Oprandi from the University of Sussex e-learning team for their fascinating insights and passion for improving Moodle's user experience and responsive design, much of which has improved my thinking and helped shape this book.

Bas Brands, Stuart Lamour, and David Scotson for their amazing work on the initial Bootstrap theme for Moodle, a project to which I am immensely proud to have contributed and to have seen make it into Moodle Core.

For general advice and conversations about mobile learning and Moodle during the writing of this book: Craig Taylor, Lesley Price, Nitin Parmar, Ross McKenzie, John Foord, Dan Jeffries, Lewis Carr, and Rob Englebright.

To my reviewers, whose valuable feedback and supportive comments lifted my spirits at the end of the laborious writing process.

And finally to my wife Rachel for putting up with my long nights while I was writing this book. And to my children Molly, George, and Cooper for sleeping soundly throughout. Love to you all.

About the Reviewers

Anthony Borrow, S.J. is a Jesuit of the New Orleans Province who has been active in the Moodle community since 2005. Anthony has an MA in Counseling from Saint Louis University and a Masters of Divinity from the Jesuit School of Theology of Santa Clara University. Anthony has worked on the design and implementation of various database systems since 1992.

Anthony serves the Moodle community as plugins facilitator. In that role, Anthony has presented at various MoodleMoots across the United States, in Australia, and at the iMoot. Anthony has taught at Dallas Jesuit College Preparatory and Cristo Rey Jesuit in Houston, Texas. He provides technical advice to the Jesuit Virtual Learning Academy (http://jvla.org/). Anthony is currently serving as Associate Pastor of Immaculate Conception Church (http://iccabq.org/) in Albuquerque, New Mexico.

Anthony wrote a series of spiritual reflections based on the spiritual exercises of Saint Ignatius entitled Toward Greater Freedom. These reflections are available at http://towardgreaterfreedom.com/index.html. Anthony co-authored the chapter on Honduras in the book *Teen Gangs: A Global View*. Anthony has also served as the technical reviewer of various other books on Moodle.

Anthony is passionate about Moodle and the use of open source educational tools to help make education available to all. He finds inspiration in the Moodle community and enjoys working with others to help them share their creativity and expertise with the larger Moodle community. Anthony greatly enjoys being part of the Moodle community where every voice contributes to advancing the use of Moodle in a variety of settings around the world.

Silvina P. Hillar is an Italian who has been teaching English since 1993. She has always had a great interest in teaching, writing, and composing techniques, and has made a lot of research on this subject. She has been investigating and using mind mapping for more than 10 years in order to embed it into teaching.

She is an English teacher, a Certified Legal Translator (English/Spanish), and has a Post Degree in Education (graduated with Honors).

She has been working in several schools and institutes with native English speaking students, and as an independent consultant for many international companies as an interpreter, translator, and VLE (Virtual Learning Environment) course designer.

She has always had a passion for technological devices and their potential application to education. Videos and cassettes were a requirement in her teaching lessons; computer use was—and still is—present. Her brother, Gastón C. Hillar, designed some programs and games for her teaching. Currently, she is teaching using Moodle and Web 2.0. She believes that one of the most amazing challenges in education is bridging the gap between classic education and modern technologies.

She has been doing a lot of research on multimedia assets that enhance teaching and learning through VLE platforms. She tries to embed students' learning through new resources that are appealing and innovative for them. Thus, multimedia stimulates different thinking skills as well as multiple intelligences.

She has authored three books by Packt Publishing, which are *Moodle 1.9: The English Teacher's Cookbook*, *Moodle 2 Multimedia Cookbook*, and *MindMapping with FreeMind*.

I would like to dedicate this book to my wonderful son, Nico.

Ben Reynolds is a Senior Program Manager of CTYOnline at The Johns Hopkins University's Center for Talented Youth (CTY, `http://cty.jhu.edu`). An award-winning fictionist, he began CTY's face-to-face writing program in 1978 and launched CTYOnline's writing program in 1983. He began administrating CTYOnline's writing and language arts division in 1985. CTYOnline serves over 13,000 students a year in writing/language arts, math, science, computer science, Advanced Placement, and foreign languages.

In the 1990s, Ben left the classroom for full-time administration both of CTY's writing/language arts program and of a residential site for CTY Summer Programs. Ben has also taught writing and the teaching of writing for the Johns Hopkins School of Continuing Studies. He holds a BA from Duke University, where he part-timed in the computer center, trading print out for punched cards, and an MA from Johns Hopkins in Fiction Writing. He is an active member of the Using Moodle community.

Ben has also had his hands in the hardware. With his second son, he built his own PCs between the mid 90s and last year, when he settled on a plain vanilla laptop. He has been technical reviewer of two books by Packt Publishing: *Moodle 2 for Teaching 7-14 Year Olds Beginner's Guide* and *Moodle 1.9 Top Extensions Cookbook*. He believes that spending 99 percent of the time uninstalling and reinstalling is just wrong.

www.PacktPub.com

Support files, eBooks, discount offers and more

You might want to visit www.PacktPub.com for support files and downloads related to your book.

Did you know that Packt offers eBook versions of every book published, with PDF and ePub files available? You can upgrade to the eBook version at www.PacktPub.com and as a print book customer, you are entitled to a discount on the eBook copy. Get in touch with us at service@packtpub.com for more details.

At www.PacktPub.com, you can also read a collection of free technical articles, sign up for a range of free newsletters and receive exclusive discounts and offers on Packt books and eBooks.

http://PacktLib.PacktPub.com

Do you need instant solutions to your IT questions? PacktLib is Packt's online digital book library. Here, you can access, read and search across Packt's entire library of books.

Why Subscribe?

- Fully searchable across every book published by Packt
- Copy and paste, print and bookmark content
- On demand and accessible via web browser

Free Access for Packt account holders

If you have an account with Packt at www.PacktPub.com, you can use this to access PacktLib today and view nine entirely free books. Simply use your login credentials for immediate access.

Table of Contents

Preface	**1**
Chapter 1: Developing Your Mobile Learning Strategy	**7**
What is mobile learning?	**7**
The capabilities of mobile devices	**8**
Warning – it's not about delivering courses	**9**
Your mobile learning strategy	**10**
Who are your learners?	10
How do your learners use their devices?	11
Mobile usage in your organization	**13**
Mobile usage in school	13
Mobile usage in further and higher education	14
Mobile usage in apprenticeships	17
Mobile usage in the workplace	18
Mobile usage in distance learning	18
Case studies	**19**
University of Sussex	20
Open University	23
Summary	**24**
Chapter 2: Setting Up Moodle for Mobile Learning	**25**
Introducing the Bootstrap and Clean themes	**25**
Introducing Moodle's Mobile apps	**26**
Setting up the Clean theme	**27**
Exploring the Clean theme	**29**
Setting up the Bootstrap theme	**32**
Setting up the Moodle Mobile app	**37**
Exploring the Moodle Mobile app	**39**
Third-party Moodle apps	**41**

Add help and support guides by using the Book module	43
Add a link to help and support from the header bar	47
Summary	49
Chapter 3: Delivering Static Content to Mobiles	**51**
Setting up file downloads	51
Learner view of file downloads	54
Setting up an eBook or App library	56
Learner view of a library	58
Using QR codes in courses	59
Building a multidevice SCORM resource	61
Adding a multidevice SCORM resource into Moodle	62
Case study – using a multidevice SCORM resource for information security awareness training	68
Using cohorts to deliver performance-support resources	69
Using a glossary for staff induction	74
Using a glossary for best practice resource collection	80
Using levels to engage new starters	81
Summary	86
Chapter 4: Delivering Multimedia Content to Mobiles	**87**
Setting up a podcast	87
Learner view of podcasts	90
Audio add-on	91
Providing audio instructions	91
Providing an audio feedback file	92
Delivering Lecturecasts to mobiles	97
Creating a video lesson	99
Summary	108
Chapter 5: Submitting Audio, Video, and Image Assignments	**109**
Creating an assignment brief for offline viewing	110
Setting up an assignment for file submission	110
Submitting a file assignment	112
Setting up a Database assignment	122
Learner submission of a Database assignment	126
Summary	130
Chapter 6: Using Mobiles for Capturing Reflective Logs and Journals	**131**
Setting up a reflective log using assignment	131
Submitting a reflective log using assignment	134
Grading a reflective log using assignment	136

Setting up a reflective log using individual forums   **139**
Submitting a reflective log using individual forums   **140**
Reviewing a reflective log using individual forums   **142**
Setting up Moodle for course blogs   **143**
Submitting a course blog post   **145**
Adding a Blogs link to the site header   **146**
Enabling portfolio export   **148**
Exporting your work to a portfolio   **149**
Summary   **151**

Chapter 7: Performing Assessments Using Mobiles   **153**
  Creating a quiz for formative assessment   **153**
    Setting up the quiz   154
    Building a question bank   158
    Building your quiz   160
    Accessing your quiz   162
    Performing a skills gap analysis   166
  Creating a quiz for summative assessment   **173**
    Setting up the quiz   174
    Accessing your quiz   175
  Checking grades   **178**
  Summary   **180**

Chapter 8: Communicating with Mobile Users   **181**
  Setting up a group discussion   **181**
    Learner view of group discussion   185
  Communicating through social networks   **186**
    Adding a Google+ contact badge   187
    Twitter hashtag feeds   188
      Setting up a Twitter hashtag feed   188
  Managing the backchannel   **192**
    Using Twitter backchannels   192
    Using Moodle chat backchannels   193
  Using Moodle messaging   **194**
    Sending a message via the Moodle Mobile app   195
    Adding a messaging link to the site header   196
    Sending SMS notifications   197
  Setting up a real-time chat session   **198**
    Participating in a chat session   199

Setting up a virtual classroom plugin   **201**
  Setting up a virtual classroom session   202
Joining a web conference   **205**
Summary   **207**
Appendix   **209**
Index   **211**

Preface

Mobile devices have become ubiquitous, and both smartphones and tablets offer so many new possibilities for learning. Moodle is gradually becoming more mobile-friendly, with the inclusion of a mobile theme in Moodle 2, the availability of responsive third-party themes, and the launch of an official Moodle app. Moodle and mobile are coming together and this opens up a new world of possibilities for teachers, instructors, and training professionals.

This book is a hands-on guide that provides you with practical ideas and step-by-step exercises that will help you to take advantage of mobile devices in your Moodle course designs, as well as providing you with an understanding of mobile learning theory so that you can create your own effective mobile learning interactions.

You will learn how to develop your mobile learning strategy and decide whether to use a mobile-friendly Moodle theme or a Moodle Mobile app to deliver this strategy. There are some types of learning activities that are perfectly suited to mobile delivery. We will look at delivering podcasts, engaging with social media, setting up photo, video, and audio assignments, setting up e-book and app libraries, uploading audio assignment feedback, submitting reflective logs, using chat and messaging tools, using web conferencing, and much more.

Mobile devices already form the backbone of learners' daily lives. If you want to use Moodle to bring those devices into the learning process, then this book is for you.

What this book covers

Chapter 1, Developing Your Mobile Learning Strategy, will aim to give you an understanding of the key concepts in mobile learning so that you can apply these to enhance your own Moodle courses . It also provides you with a vision of how Moodle for mobile learning can be put to use in your own organization.

Chapter 2, Setting Up Moodle for Mobile Learning, will help you to get your Moodle site set up so that it can be used for mobile learning, introduces the mobile-friendly themes that ship with Moodle, and explores the official Moodle Mobile app.

Chapter 3, Delivering Static Content to Mobiles, will look at how to deliver static content (that does not involve the use of multimedia) from Moodle to mobile devices.

Chapter 4, Delivering Multimedia Content to Mobiles, will cover how to deliver multimedia content from Moodle to mobile devices.

Chapter 5, Submitting Audio, Video, and Image Assignments, will explore an important element of mobile learning: using the built-in audio recording and camera capabilities of the mobile devices in students' pockets to allow them to capture audio, photos, or videos and upload these into Moodle for sharing or grading.

Chapter 6, Using Mobiles for Capturing Reflective Logs and Journals, will look at the use of reflective logs and journals for knowledge capture on mobile devices, the shorter nature of these activities lending themselves well to production on a tablet or even a smartphone.

Chapter 7, Performing Assessments Using Mobiles, will explain how a number of different types of assessment tools can built in Moodle by using the quiz activity, and how these can be optimized for mobile learning.

Chapter 8, Communicating with Mobile Users, will cover the wide range of communication tools that come with Moodle, and explores how these can be used in a mobile learning context.

Appendix, has a list of reference links that will help you to dig deeper into merging Moodle with your mobile device.

What you need for this book

Mobile support in Moodle depends on the version of Moodle you are using. At a minimum you will require Moodle 2.2, which was the first version to officially have any level of mobile support.

Who this book is for

This book is primarily aimed at Moodle course practitioners—teachers, tutors, instructors, and learning and development professionals. The book concentrates on understanding how the features and capabilities of mobile devices can be taken advantage of in your Moodle course design. There is just a single section on setting up Moodle for mobile delivery, which is aimed more at Moodle administrators. However, this book will also be useful for course practitioners who need to influence their IT team to make any required system changes. The book does not require any prior knowledge of mobile technology or the capabilities of the latest smartphones. Indeed, by the end of the book you will realize that *anyone* can deliver great courses that allow their learners to interact with their courses using the mobile devices in their pockets.

Conventions

In this book, you will find a number of styles of text that distinguish between different kinds of information. Here are some examples of these styles, and an explanation of their meaning.

Code words in text, database table names, folder names, filenames, file extensions, pathnames, dummy URLs, user input, and Twitter handles are shown as follows: "Copy the `bootstrap` folder into your `<moodle site>/theme` folder."

New terms and **important words** are shown in bold. Words that you see on the screen, in menus or dialog boxes for example, appear in the text like this: "On the **ADMINISTRATION** block, navigate to **Site administration | Appearance | Themes | Theme selector**."

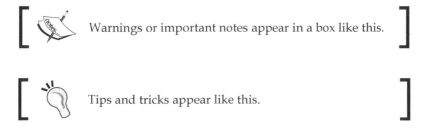

Warnings or important notes appear in a box like this.

Tips and tricks appear like this.

Reader feedback

Feedback from our readers is always welcome. Let us know what you think about this book—what you liked or may have disliked. Reader feedback is important for us to develop titles that you really get the most out of.

To send us general feedback, simply send an e-mail to `feedback@packtpub.com`, and mention the book title via the subject of your message.

If there is a topic that you have expertise in and you are interested in either writing or contributing to a book, see our author guide on `www.packtpub.com/authors`.

Customer support

Now that you are the proud owner of a Packt book, we have a number of things to help you to get the most from your purchase.

Errata

Although we have taken every care to ensure the accuracy of our content, mistakes do happen. If you find a mistake in one of our books—maybe a mistake in the text or the code—we would be grateful if you would report this to us. By doing so, you can save other readers from frustration and help us improve subsequent versions of this book. If you find any errata, please report them by visiting `http://www.packtpub.com/submit-errata`, selecting your book, clicking on the **errata submission form** link, and entering the details of your errata. Once your errata are verified, your submission will be accepted and the errata will be uploaded on our website, or added to any list of existing errata, under the Errata section of that title. Any existing errata can be viewed by selecting your title from `http://www.packtpub.com/support`.

Piracy

Piracy of copyright material on the Internet is an ongoing problem across all media. At Packt, we take the protection of our copyright and licenses very seriously. If you come across any illegal copies of our works, in any form, on the Internet, please provide us with the location address or website name immediately so that we can pursue a remedy.

Please contact us at copyright@packtpub.com with a link to the suspected pirated material.

We appreciate your help in protecting our authors, and our ability to bring you valuable content.

Questions

You can contact us at questions@packtpub.com if you are having a problem with any aspect of the book, and we will do our best to address it.

1
Developing Your Mobile Learning Strategy

This chapter aims to provide you with a vision of how Moodle for mobile learning can be put to use in your own organization. It will give you an understanding of the foundations of mobile learning, some insights into how important mobile learning is becoming, and how it is gaining momentum in different sectors. At the end of the chapter, you should have an understanding of the key concepts of mobile learning so that you can apply these concepts in order to enhance your own Moodle courses. We want to set you off on a mobile learning path that will allow you to better meet the needs and expectations of your learners who, as we will see, already use mobile devices as the backbone of their daily online interactions, and expect mobile compatibility to be the norm.

In this chapter, we will look at the following:

- Background to mobile learning
- Background to mobile devices
- The 4 Cs of mobile learning
- Your mobile learning strategy
- Understanding your learners and how they use their devices
- Mobile usage in industry

What is mobile learning?

There have been many attempts at defining mobile learning. Is it learning done on the move, such as on a laptop while we sit in a train? Or is it learning done on a personal mobile device, such as a smartphone or a tablet?

While there are a number of definitions available, for this book we are taking our cue from the eLearning Guild's 2007 definition, which seems the most sensible:

> *"Any activity that allows individuals to be more productive when consuming, interacting with, or creating information, mediated through a compact digital portable device that the individual carries on a regular basis, has reliable connectivity, and fits in a pocket or purse."*

This covers a range of device types, including feature phones, smartphones, portable gaming devices, media players, e-readers, and tablets. What it does *not* cover though, are netbooks and laptops which, although they can clearly be used while the user is mobile, offer a more traditional desktop-based computing experience.

The capabilities of mobile devices

Anyone can develop mobile learning. You don't need to be a gadget geek or have the latest smartphone or tablet. You certainly don't need to know *anything* about the make and models of devices on the market. The only thing the learning practitioner really needs is an understanding of the capabilities of the mobile devices that your learners have. This will inform the types of mobile learning interventions that will be best suited to your audience. The following table shows an overview of what a mobile learner might be able to do with each of the device types. The Device uses column on the left should already be setting off lots of great learning ideas in your head!

Device uses	Feature phone	Smartphone	Tablet	Gaming device	Media player
Send texts	Yes	Yes			
Make calls	Yes	Yes			
Take photos	Yes	Yes	Yes	Yes	Yes
Listen to music	Yes	Yes	Yes	Yes	Yes
Social networking	Yes	Yes	Yes	Yes	Yes
Take high res photos		Yes	Yes	Yes	Yes
Web searches		Yes	Yes	Yes	Yes
Web browsing		Yes	Yes	Yes	Yes
Watch online videos		Yes	Yes	Yes	Yes
Video calls		Yes	Yes	Yes	Yes
Edit photos		Yes	Yes	Yes	Yes
Shoot videos		Yes	Yes		Yes
Take audio recordings		Yes	Yes		Yes

Device uses	Feature phone	Smartphone	Tablet	Gaming device	Media player
Install apps		Yes	Yes		Yes
Edit documents		Yes	Yes		Yes
Use maps		Yes	Yes		Yes
Send MMS		Yes	Yes		
View catch-up TV			Yes	Yes	
Better quality web browsing			Yes	Yes	
Shopping online			Yes		
Trip planning			Yes		

Bear in mind that screen size will also impact the type of learning activity that can be undertaken. For example:

- Feature phone displays are very small, so learning activities for this device type should center on text messaging with a tutor or capturing photos for an assignment.

- Smartphones are significantly larger so there is a much wider range of learning activities available, especially around the creation of material such as photo and video for assignment or portfolio purposes, and a certain amount of web searching and browsing.

- Tablets are more akin to the desktop computing environment, although some tasks such as typing are harder and taking photos is bit clumsier due to the larger size of the device. They are great for short learning tasks, assessments, video watching, and much more.

Warning – it's not about delivering courses

Mobile learning can be many things. What it is *not* is simply the delivery of e-learning courses, which is traditionally the domain of the desktop computer, on a smaller device. Of course it can be used to deliver educational materials, but what is more important is that it can also be used to foster collaboration, to facilitate communication, to access performance support, and to capture evidence. But if you try to deliver an entire course purely on a mobile, then the likelihood is that no one will use it.

Your mobile learning strategy

Finding a starting point for your mobile learning design is easier said than done. It is often useful when designing any type of online interaction to think through a few typical user types and build up a picture of who they are and what they want to use the system for. This helps you to visualize who you are designing for. In addition to this, in order to understand how best to utilize mobile devices for learning, you also need to understand how people actually *use* their mobile devices. For example, learners are highly unlikely to sit at a smartphone and complete a 60 minutes e-learning course or type out an essay. But they are very likely to read an article, do some last minute test preparation or communicate with other learners.

Who are your learners?

Understanding your users is an important part of designing online experiences. You should take time to understand the types of learners within your own organization and what their mobile usage looks like, as a first step in delivering mobile learning on Moodle. With this in mind, let's look at a handful of typical mobile learners from around the world who could reasonably be expected to be using an educational or workplace learning platform such as Moodle:

- Maria is an office manager in Madrid, Spain. She doesn't leave home without her smartphone and uses it wherever she is, whether for e-mail, web searching and browsing, reading the news, or social networking. She lives in a country where smartphone penetration has reached almost half of the population, of whom two-third access the internet every day on their mobile. The company she works for has a small learning platform for delivery of work-based learning activities and performance support resources.

- Fourteen year old Jennifer attends school in Rio de Janeiro, Brazil. Like many of her peers, she carries a smartphone with her and it's a key part of her life. The Brazilian population is one of the most connected in the developing world with nearly half of the population using the Internet, and its mobile phone subscriptions accounting for one-third of the entire subscriptions across Latin America and the Caribbean. Her elementary school uses a learning platform for the delivery of course resources, formative assessments, and submission of student assignments.

- Nineteen year old Mike works as an apprentice at a large car maker in Sunderland, UK. He spends about one-third of his time in formal education, and his remaining days each week are spent on the production line, getting a thorough grounding in every element of the car manufacturing process. He owns a smartphone and uses it heavily, in a country where nearly half of the population accesses the Internet at least monthly on their smartphone. His employer has a learning platform for delivery of work-based learning and his college also has their own platform where he keeps a training diary and uploads evidence of skills acquisition for later submission and marking.

- Josh is a twenty year old university student in the United States. In his country, nearly 90 percent of adults now own a mobile phone and half of all adults use their phone to access the Internet, although in his age group this increases to three quarters. Among his student peers across the U.S., 40 percent are already doing test preparation on their mobiles, whether their institution provides the means or not. His university uses a learning platform for delivery of course resources, submission of student assignments, and student collaborative activities.

These four particular learners were not chosen at random—there is one important thing that connects them all. The four countries they are from represent not just important mobile markets but, according to the statistics page on `Moodle.org`, also represent the four largest Moodle territories, together making up over a third of all registered Moodle sites in the world.

When you combine those Moodle market statistics with the level of mobile internet usage in each country, you can immediately see why support for mobile learning is so important for Moodle sites.

How do your learners use their devices?

In 2012, Google published the findings of a research survey which investigated how users behave across computer, tablet, smartphone, and TV screens. Their researchers found that users make decisions about what device to use for a given task depending on four elements that together make up the user's context: location, goal, available time, and attitude. Each of these is important to take into account when thinking about what sort of learning interactions your users could engage in when using their mobile devices, and you should be aiming to offer a range of mobile learning interactions that can lend themselves to different contexts, for example, offering tasks ranging in length from 2 to 20 minutes, and tasks suited to different locations, such as home, work, college, or out in the field. The attitude element is an interesting one, and it's important to allow learners to choose tasks that are appropriate to their mood at the time.

Google also found that users either move between screens to perform a single task (*sequential screening*) or use multiple screens at the same time (*simultaneous screening*). In the case of simultaneous screening, they are likely to be performing complementary tasks relating to the same activity on each screen. From a learning point of view, you can design for multi-screen tasks. For example, you may find learners use their computer to perform some complex research and then collect evidence in the field using their smartphone—these would be sequential screening tasks. A media studies student could be watching a rolling news channel on the television while taking photos, video, and notes for an assignment on his tablet or smartphone—these would be simultaneous screening tasks.

Understanding the different scenarios in which learners can use multiple screens will open up new opportunities for mobile learning.

A key statement from the Google research states that "Smartphones are the backbone of our daily media interactions". However, despite occupying such a dominant position in our lives, the smartphone also accounts for the lowest time per user interaction at an average of 17 minutes, as opposed to 30 minutes for tablet, 39 minutes for computer, and 43 minutes for TV. This is an important point to bear in mind when designing mobile learning: as a rule of thumb you can expect a learner to engage with a tablet-based task for half an hour, and a smartphone-based task for just a quarter of an hour.

Google helpfully outlines some important multi-screen lessons. While these are aimed at identifying consumer behavior and in particular online shopping habits, we can interpret them for use in mobile learning as follows:

- Understand how people consume digital media and tailor your learning strategies to each channel
- Learning goals should be adjusted to account for the inherent differences in each device
- Learners must be able to save their progress between devices
- Learners must be able to easily find the learning platform (Moodle) on each device
- Once in the learning platform, it must be easy for learners to find what they are looking for quickly
- Smartphones are the backbone of your learners' daily media use, so design your learning to be started on smartphone and continued on a tablet or desktop computer

Having an understanding of how modern-day learners use their different screens and devices will have a real impact on your learning design.

Mobile usage in your organization

In 2011, the world reached a technology watershed when it was estimated that one third of the world's seven billion people were online. The growth in online users is dominated by the developing world and is fuelled by mobile devices. There are now a staggering six billion mobile phone subscriptions globally. Mobile technology has quite simply become ubiquitous. And as Google showed us, people use mobile devices as the backbone of their daily media consumption, and most people already use them for school, college, or work regardless of whether they are allowed to.

In this section, we will look at how mobiles are used in some of the key sectors in which Moodle is used: in schools, further and higher education, and in the workplace.

Mobile usage in school

Moodle is widely used throughout primary and secondary education, and mobile usage among school pupils is widespread. The two are natural bedfellows in this sector. For example, in the UK half of all 12 to 15 year olds own a smartphone while 70 percent of 8 to 15 year olds have a games console such as a Nintendo DS or PlayStation in their bedroom.

Mobile device use is quite simply rampant among school children. Many primary schools now have policies which allow children to bring mobile phones into school, recognizing that such devices have a role to play in helping pupils feel safe and secure, particularly on the journey to and from school. However, it is a fairly normal practice among this age group for mobiles to be handed in at the start of the school day and collected at the end of the day. For primary pupils, therefore, the use of mobile devices for education will be largely for homework.

In secondary schools, the picture is very different. There is not likely to be a device hand-in policy during school hours and a variety of acceptable use policies will be in use. An acceptable use policy may include a provision for using mobiles in lesson time, with a teacher's agreement, for the purposes of supporting learning. This, of course, opens up valuable learning opportunities.

Mobile learning in education has been the subject of a number of initiatives and research studies which are all excellent sources of information. These include:

- Learning2Go, who were pioneers in mobile learning for schools in the UK, distributing hundreds of Windows Mobile devices to Wolverhampton schools between 2003 and 2007, introducing smartphones in 2008 under the Computers for Pupils initiative and the national MoLeNET scheme.

- Learning Untethered, which was not a formal research project but an exploration that gave Android tablets to a class of fifth graders. It was noted that the overall "feel" of the classroom shifted as students took a more active role in discovery, exploration and active learning.

- The Dudley Handhelds initiative, which provided 300 devices to learners in grade five to ten across six primary schools, one secondary special school, and one mainstream secondary school.

These are just a few of the many research studies available, and they are well worth a read to understand how schools have been implementing mobile learning for different age groups.

Mobile usage in further and higher education

College students are heavy users of mobiles, and there is a roughly half and half split between smartphones and feature phones among the student community. Of the smartphone users, over 80 percent use them for college-related tasks. As we saw from Google's research, smartphones are the backbone of your learners' daily media use for those who have them. So if you don't already provide mobile learning opportunities on your Moodle site, then it is likely that your users are already helping themselves to the vast array of mobile learning sites and apps that have sprung up in recent years to meet the high demand for such services.

 If you don't provide your students with mobile learning opportunities, you can bet your bottom dollar that someone else is, and it could be of dubious quality or out of date.

Despite the ubiquity of the mobile, many schools and colleges continue to ban them, viewing mobiles as a distraction or a means of bullying. They are fighting a rising tide, however.

Students are living their lives through their mobile devices, and these devices have become their primary means of communication. A study in late 2012 of nearly 295,000 students found that despite e-mail, IM, and text messaging being the dominant peer-communication tools for students, less than half of 14 to 18 year olds and only a quarter of 11 to 14 year olds used them to communicate with their teachers. Over half of high school students said they would use their smartphone to communicate with their teacher if it was allowed.

Unfortunately it rarely is, but this will change. Students want to be able to communicate electronically with their teachers; they want online textbooks with classmate collaboration tools; they want to go online on their mobile to get information.

Go to where your students are and communicate with them in their native environment, which is via their mobile. Be there for them, engage them, and inspire them.

In the years approaching 2010, some higher education institutions started engaging in headline-grabbing "iPad for every student" initiatives. Many institutions adopted a quick-win strategy of making mobile-friendly websites with access to campus information, directories, news and events. It is estimated that in the USA over 90 percent of higher education institutions have mobile-friendly websites. Some of the headline-grabbing initiatives include the following:

- Seton Hill University was the first to roll out iPads to all full-time students in 2010 and have continued to do so every year since. They are at the forefront of mobile learning in the US University sector and use Moodle as their virtual learning environment (VLE).

- Abilene Christian University was the first university in the U.S. to provide iPhones or iPod Touches to all new full-time students in 2008, and are regarded as one of the most mobile-friendly campuses in the U.S.

- The University of Western Sydney in Australia will roll out 11,000 iPads to all faculty and newly-enrolled students in 2013, as well as creating their own mobile apps.

- Coventry University in the UK is creating a smart campus in which the geographical location of students triggers access to content and experiences through their mobile devices.

- MoLeNET in the UK was one of the world's largest mobile learning implementations, comprising 115 colleges, 29 schools, 50,000 students, and 4,000 staff from 2007 to 2010. This was a research-led initiative although unfortunately the original website has now been taken down.

While some of these examples are about providing mobile devices to new students, the Bring Your Own Device (BYOD) trend is strong in further and higher education. We know that mobile devices form the backbone of students' media consumption and in the U.S. alone, 75 percent of students use their phone to access the Internet. Additionally, 40 percent have signed up to online test preparation sites on their mobiles, heavily suggesting that if an institution doesn't provide mobile learning services, students will go and get it elsewhere anyway.

Instead of the glamorous offer of iPads for all, some institutions have chosen to invest heavily in their wireless network infrastructure in support of a BYOD approach. This is a very heavy investment and can be far more expensive than a few thousand iPads. Some BYOD implementations include:

- King's College London in the UK, which supports 6,000 staff and 23,500 students

- The University of Tennessee at Knoxville in the U.S., which hosts more than 26,000 students and 5,000 faculty and staff members, with nearly 75,000 smartphones, tablets, and laptops

- The University of South Florida in the U.S., which supports 40,000 users

- Sau Paolo State University in Brazil, which has 45,000 students and noted that despite providing desktop machines in the computer labs, half of all students opted to use their own devices instead

There are many challenges to BYOD which are not within the scope of this book, but there are also many resources on how to implement a BYOD policy that minimizes such risks. Use the Internet to seek these out.

Providing campus information websites on mobiles obviously was not the key rationale behind such technology investments. The real interest is in delivering mobile learning, and this remains an area full of experimentation and research. Google Scholar can be used to chart the rise of mobile learning research and it becomes evident how this really takes off in the second half of the decade, when the first major institutions started investing in mobile technology. It indexes scholarly literature, including journal and conference papers, theses and dissertations, academic books, pre-prints, abstracts, and technical reports. A year-by-year search reveals the rise of mobile learning research from just over 100 articles in 2000 to over 6,000 in 2012.

The following chart depicts the rise of mobile learning in academic research:

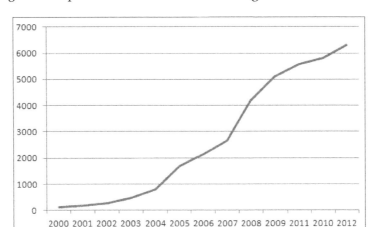

Mobile usage in apprenticeships

A typical apprenticeship will include a significant amount of college-based learning towards a qualification, alongside a major component based in the workplace under the supervision of an employer while the apprentice learns a particular trade. Due to the movement of the student from college to workplace, and the fact that the apprentice usually has to keep a reflective log and capture evidence of their skills acquisition, mobile devices can play a really useful role in apprenticeships.

Traditionally, the age group for apprenticeships is 16 to 24 year olds. This is an age group that has never known a world without mobiles and their mobile devices are integrated into the fabric of their daily lives and media consumption. They use social networks, SMS, and instant messaging rather than e-mail, and are more likely to use the mobile internet than any other age group. Statistics from the U.S. reveal that 75 percent of students use their phone to access the Internet.

Reflective logs are an important part of any apprenticeship. There are a number of activities in Moodle that can be used for keeping reflective logs, and these are ideal for mobile learning. Reflective log entries tend to be shorter than traditional assignments and lend themselves well to production on a tablet or even a smartphone. Consumption of reflective logs is perfect for both smartphone and tablet devices, as posts tend to be readable in less than 5 minutes.

Many institutions use Moodle coupled with an ePortfolio tool such as Mahara or Onefile to manage apprenticeship programs. There are additional Packt Publishing books on ePortfolio tools such as Mahara, should you wish to investigate a third-party, open source ePortfolio solution.

Mobile usage in the workplace

BYOD in the workplace is also becoming increasingly common, and, appears to be an unstoppable trend. It may also be discouraged or banned on security, data protection, or distraction grounds, but it is happening regardless. There is an increasing amount of research available on this topic, and some key findings from various studies reveal the scale of the trend:

- A survey of 600 IT and business leaders revealed that 90 percent of survey respondents had employees using their own devices at work

- 65 to 75 percent of companies allow some sort of BYOD usage

- 80 to 90 percent of employees use a personal mobile device for business use

If you are a workplace learning practitioner then you need to sit up and take note of these numbers if you haven't done so already. Even if your organization doesn't officially have a BYOD policy, it is most likely that your employees are already using their own mobile devices for business purposes. It's up to your IT department to manage this safely, and again there are many resources and case studies available online to help with this. But as a learning practitioner, whether it's officially supported or not, it's worth asking yourself whether you should embrace it anyway, and provide learning activities to these users and their devices.

Mobile usage in distance learning

Online distance learning is principally used in higher education (HE), and many institutions have taken to it either as a new stream of revenue or as a way of building their brand globally. Enrolments have rocketed over recent years; the number of U.S. students enrolled in an online course has increased from one to six million in a decade. Online enrolments have also been the greatest source of new enrolments in HE in that time, outperforming general student enrolment dramatically. Indeed, the year 2011 in the US saw a 10 percent growth rate in distance learning enrolment against 2 percent in the overall HE student population. In the 2010 to 2011 academic years, online enrolments accounted for 31 percent of all U.S. HE enrolments.

Against this backdrop of phenomenal growth in HE distance learning courses, we also have a new trend of Massive Online Open Courses (MOOCs) which aim to extend enrolment past traditional student populations to the vast numbers of potential students for whom a formal HE program of study may not be an option.

The convenience and flexibility of distance learning appeal to certain groups of the population. Distance learners are likely to be older students, with more than 30 years of age being the dominant age group. They are also more likely to be in full-time employment and taking the course to help advance their careers, and are highly likely to be married and juggling home and family commitments with their jobs and coursework.

We know that among the 30 to 40 age group mobile device use is very high, particularly among working professionals, who are a major proportion of HE distance learners. However, the MOOC audience is of real interest here as this audience is much more diverse. As many MOOC users find traditional HE programs out of their reach, many of these will be in developing countries, where we already know that users are leapfrogging desktop computing and going straight to mobile devices and wireless connectivity. For these types of courses, mobile support is absolutely crucial.

A wide variety of tools exist to support online distance learning, and these are split between synchronous and asynchronous tools, although typically a blend of the two is used. In synchronous learning, all participants are present at the same time. Courses will therefore be organized to a timetable, and will involve tools such as webinars, video conferences, and real-time chat. In asynchronous learning, courses are self-directed and students work to their own schedules, and tools include e-mail, discussion forums, audio recording, video recordings, and printed material.

Connecting distance learning from traditional institutions to MOOCs is a recognized need to improve course quality and design, faculty training, course assessment, and student retention. There are known barriers, including motivation, feedback, teacher contact, and student isolation. These are major challenges to the effectiveness of distance learning, and later in this book we will demonstrate how mobile devices can be used to address some of these areas.

Case studies

The following case studies illustrate two approaches to how an HE institution and a distance learning institution have adopted Moodle to deliver mobile learning. Both institutions were very early movers in making Moodle mobile-friendly, and can be seen as torch bearers for the rest of us. Fortunately, both institutions have also been influential in the approach that Moodle HQ have taken to mobile compatibility, so in using the new mobile features in recent versions of Moodle, we are all able to take advantage of the substantial amount of work that went into these two sites.

University of Sussex

The University of Sussex is a research-led HE institution on the south coast of England. They use a customized Moodle 1.9 installation called **Study Direct**, which plays host to 1,500 editing tutors and 15,000 students across 2,100 courses per year, and receives 13,500 unique hits per day.

The e-learning team at the University of Sussex contains five staff (one manager, two developers, one user support, and one tutor support) whose remit covers a much wider range of learning technologies beyond the VLE. However, the team has achieved a great deal with limited resources. It has been working towards a responsive design for some years and has helped to influence the direction of Moodle with regards to designing for mobile devices and usability, through speaking at UK Moodle and HE conferences and providing passionate inputs into debates on the Moodle forums on the subject of interface design. Further to this, team member Stuart Lamour is one of the three original developers of the Bootstrap theme for Moodle, which is used throughout this book.

The Study Direct site shows what is possible in Moodle, given the time and resources for its development and a focus on user-centered design. The approach has been to avoid going down the native application route for mobile access like many institutions have done, and to instead focus on a responsive, browser-based user experience.

The login page is simple and clean. One of the nice things that the University of Sussex has done is to think through the user interactions on its site and clearly identify calls to action, typically with a green button, as shown by the **sign in** button on the login page in the following screenshot:

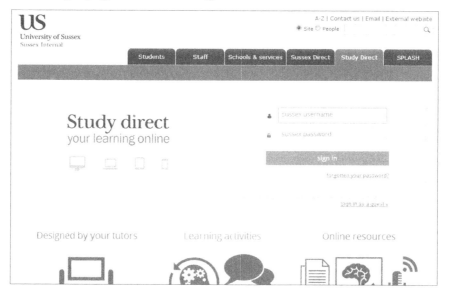

The team has built its own responsive theme for Moodle. While the team has taken a leading role on development of the Moodle 2 Bootstrap theme, the University of Sussex site is still on Moodle 1.9 so this implementation uses its own custom theme. This theme is fully responsive and looks good when viewed on a tablet or a smartphone, reordering screen elements as necessary for each screen resolution.

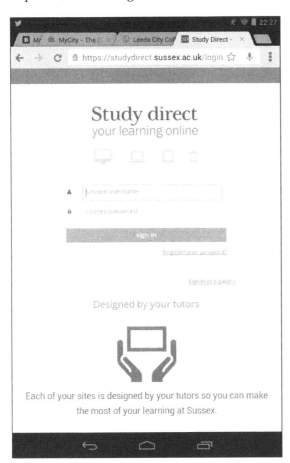

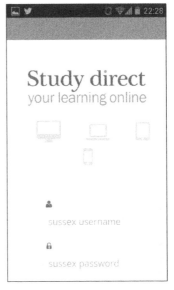

The course page, shown in the following screenshot, is similarly clear and uncluttered. The editing interface has been customized quite heavily to give tutors a clear and easy way to edit their courses without running the risk of messing up the user interface. The team maintains a useful and informative blog explaining what they have done to improve the user experience, and which is well worth a read.

Open University

The Open University (OU) in the UK runs one the largest Moodle sites in the world. It is currently using Moodle 2 for the OU's main VLE as well as for its OpenLearn and Qualifications online platforms. Its Moodle implementation regularly sees days with well over one million transactions and over 60,000 unique users, and has seen peak times of 5,000 simultaneous online users.

The OU's focus on mobile Moodle goes back to about 2010, so it was an early mover in this area. This means that the OU did not have the benefit of all the mobile-friendly features that now come with Moodle, but had to largely create its own mobile interface from scratch.

Anthony Forth gave a presentation at the UK Moodle Moot in 2011 on the OU's approach to mobile interface design for Moodle. He identified that at the time the Open University migrated to Moodle 2 in 2011 it had over 13,000 mobile users per month.

The OU chose to survey a group of 558 of these users in detail to investigate their needs more closely. It transpired that the most popular uses of Moodle on mobile devices was for forums, news, resources and study planners, while areas such as wikis and blogs were very low down the list of users' priorities. So the OU's mobile design focused on these particular areas as well as looking at usability in general.

The preceding screenshot shows the OU course page with tabbed access to the popular areas such as **Planner**, **News**, **Forums**, and **Resources**, and then the main content area providing space for latest news, unread forum posts, and activities taking place this week.

The site uses a nice, clean, and easy to understand user interface in which a lot of thought has gone into the needs of the student.

Summary

In this chapter, we have provided you with a vision of how mobile learning could be put to use on your own organization's Moodle platform. We gave you an understanding of some of the foundation concepts of mobile learning, some insights into how important mobile learning is becoming, and how it is gaining momentum in different sectors.

Your learners are already using mobile devices whether in educational institutions or in the workplace, and they use mobile devices as the backbone of their daily online interactions. They want to also use them for learning. Hopefully, we have started you off on a mobile learning path that will allow you to make this happen.

Mobile devices are where the future of Moodle is going to be played out, so it makes complete sense to be designing for mobile access right now. Fortunately, Moodle already provides the means for this to happen and provides tools that allow you to set it up for mobile delivery.

2
Setting Up Moodle for Mobile Learning

We now know why mobile learning is so important, and hopefully you are starting to have some thoughts about particular mobile learning activities that may be suitable for your organization. The next step is to get your Moodle site setup so that it can be used for mobile learning.

Mobile support in Moodle depends upon the version of Moodle you are using. At a minimum you will require Moodle 2.2, which was the first version to officially have any level of mobile support.

You may know that Moodle uses what is called **themes** to control page layouts and styles. Moodle comes with a handful of built-in themes, and you can use these on your site to achieve the look and feel that is right for you. You can even build your own themes if you have the development expertise.

Introducing the Bootstrap and Clean themes

In recent years, a mobile-friendly theme called Bootstrap was developed in the Moodle community and released as an open source theme on https://moodle.org/. Bootstrap is a responsive theme. If you haven't come across the idea of responsive web design before, it is actually very simple. It allows the developer to use the browser's built-in ability to detect the screen width and deliver different layouts for different screen widths. For example, a 1,000 pixel wide screen can support a three-column layout but this can be automatically changed to a two-column layout if the screen is under 600 pixels wide, and when it reaches the smaller smartphone width of 300 pixels then the content can be reworked into a single-column layout.

The Bootstrap theme does exactly this, and will adjust your layouts depending on the user's screen width. If you are using Moodle 2.2 through to 2.4, you can download and use the Bootstrap theme (available on `https://moodle.org/`); this chapter will show you how to do that.

The Bootstrap theme proved so popular within the Moodle community that it was actually included with Moodle 2.5, in the form of a theme called **Clean**. If you have Moodle 2.5, you simply need to enable this theme. This chapter will also show you how to do that.

A little bit of mobile Moodle history

The Bootstrap and Clean themes superseded an earlier attempt at a Moodle mobile theme, which was called **MyMobile**, and which shipped with Moodle 2.2.

MyMobile used the browser's device detection feature and passed this information to Moodle. Moodle could then be configured to deliver different themes depending on the device type. However, this became slightly problematic over time because of the mobile device convergence issue we mentioned in *Chapter 1, Developing Your Mobile Learning Strategy*. For example, there are now large and small tablets, and large and small smartphones, and the largest smartphones are pretty similar to the smallest tablets. Delivering a theme using device detection forces the same theme to a particular type of device, regardless of whether it has a large or small screen.

The mobile hardware landscape is changing so fast that it is no longer realistic to expect Moodle developers to keep changing their code to keep up with the device proliferation. Responsive themes are a far more elegant solution. Developers cannot plan for new device types that may appear in future, but they can plan for different screen resolutions.

For this reason, we excluded MyMobile from this book. It was a great first attempt at mobile support in Moodle, but has now been superseded.

Introducing Moodle's Mobile apps

Themes are good, but they don't allow you to load the site for offline use, or take advantage of smartphone features like the camera. For this you need an app. Moodle does have an official **Moodle Mobile** app. This is a HTML5 app that works on both Android and Apple devices. The developers of the app have purposely not chosen to simply recreate Moodle for a mobile device, but have selected a number of specific tasks that the learners are mostly likely to do on their mobile devices.

The Moodle Mobile app allows learners to capture and upload images, audio, and video; view course participants; and use Moodle messaging and enable push notifications. This chapter will show you how to download and set up the official Moodle app.

There are also a number of unofficial apps available in the Android and Apple app stores that could work with your Moodle site, including one that works with Moodle 1.9. We will wrap up this chapter with an overview of the alternative apps available.

A little bit more mobile Moodle history...

There is a previous version of the official Moodle app hanging around in the Apple app store. This was the first attempt at creating a native app for Moodle and was released in late 2011. It targeted Apple devices only, and there was scheduled to be another version released for Android in 2012.

However, the mobile landscape changes fast and it became apparent during 2012 that a different version for each platform was not an efficient way to develop for mobile, so a decision was taken to embark on a developing a HTML5 app that worked with *all* devices. So in July 2012, Moodle HQ changed direction and started work on a HTML5 app instead.

The HTML5 app is a continuation of the work by Moodle developer *Juan Leyva* on his **Unofficial Moodle Mobile** app, or **umm** for short (refer to the *Third-party Moodle apps* section).

Setting up the Clean theme

Role: Site Administrator	**Version**: 2.5

The Clean theme is already available on your Moodle site, and just needs to be enabled. You just need to go into the Moodle **Theme selector** screen and set it up as the default site theme.

Carry out the following steps in Moodle 2.5 for setting up the Clean theme:

1. On the **ADMINISTRATION** block, navigate to **Site administration** | **Appearance** | **Themes** | **Theme selector**.

2. This will open up the **Theme Selector** screen. There are four options listed under **Device type** that you can select: **Default**, **Legacy**, **Mobile**, and **Tablet**.

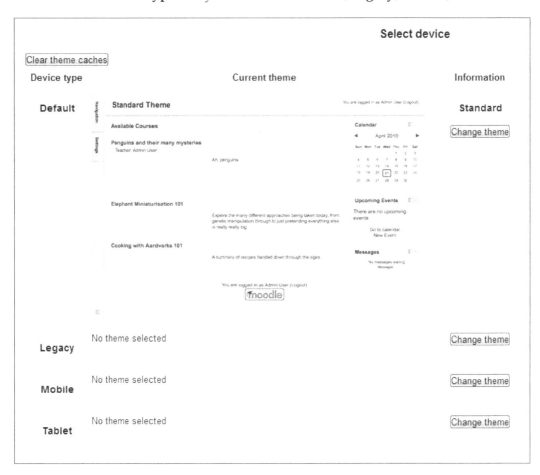

3. Click on the **Change theme** button next to the **Default device** type. On the next screen you are presented with a long list of themes, each with a screenshot. Scroll down to theme called **Clean** and click on the **Use theme** button.

4. After clicking on the **Use theme** button, a confirmation screen is displayed. This will show the Clean screenshot and some information about the theme. Click on **Continue**.

5. After clicking on **Continue** you will be taken back to the **Theme selector** screen, which will now display the newly selected Clean theme next to the **Default device** type.

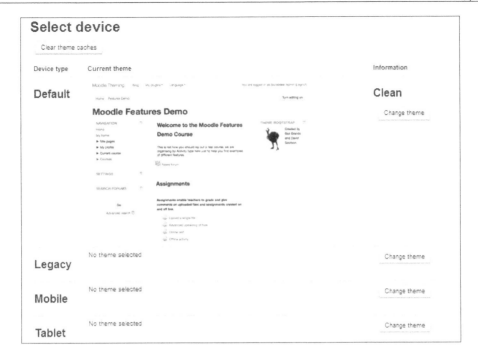

Exploring the Clean theme

The first impressions of the Clean theme are excellent. It's not only responsive; by using the styles inherited from the open source Twitter Bootstrap project (http://twitter.github.com/bootstrap) the theme has a modern and fresh design that blows a breath of fresh air into the Moodle interface.

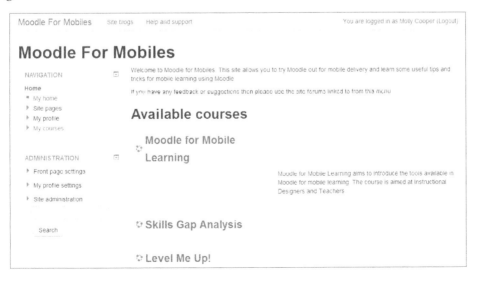

Let's take a more detailed look around the theme.

On the course pages, the breadcrumb trail looks a lot more elegant, in its own colored block, neatly tucked under the main heading.

The side blocks all have a standard light gray background color with a dark gray border, and the block headings are bold and capitalized. There is also improved spacing between the menu items.

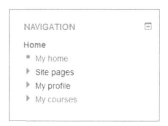

The main editing buttons are now standard colors throughout the site.

However, these are purely cosmetic changes. To see the really powerful use of this important theme, you need to resize your browser. First, make sure that your browser is not maximized, and then grab the edge of the browser with your mouse and resize it to make it narrower. Then watch what happens to the Moodle page as the browser window gets narrower and narrower.

There is a point at which the whole screen reverts to a single-column layout, and this is at about 600 pixels, which is about the size of a small tablet.

If you go right down to 300 pixels or so, to emulate a smart phone, you see something like the example shown in following screenshot, in Moodle 2.5:

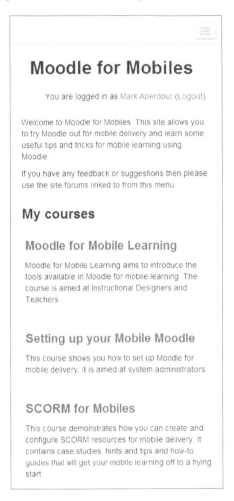

Several things have happened to the screen:

- The navigation tabs are hidden, and can be revealed by clicking on the gray icon at the top-right corner.
- The title and login/logout link are at the top, as you would expect.
- The main content/menu area is below the title and login/logout link. The menu items are no longer displayed with the title on the left and the summary on the right as previously, but are arranged vertically.
- Any side blocks are displayed underneath this.

It's a superb theme, and its beauty is in its simplicity. The intention is that it provides a base on which you can build, so if you have development skills you should be thinking about changing the color scheme at the very least, to match that of your organization's branding.

In Moodle 2.5, the **NAVIGATION** and **SETTINGS** blocks automatically move underneath the menu and content area so that the main content is displayed first. In previous versions of Moodle using the Bootstrap theme, they would be above the content area instead.

Setting up the Bootstrap theme

Role: Site Administrator	**Version**: 2.2 to 2.4

If you have Moodle 2.2, 2.3, or 2.4, you can still get all the benefits of the **Clean** theme by downloading and installing the **Bootstrap** theme on which Clean is based.

Carry out the following steps in order to download and install the Bootstrap theme:

1. First you will need to download the theme from the **Moodle Plugins Directory** page. Go to `https://moodle.org/plugins/` and type `Bootstrap` in the search box, then click on the **Search plugins** button.

2. This will bring back the result **Themes: Bootstrap**. It should look something like the following screenshot:

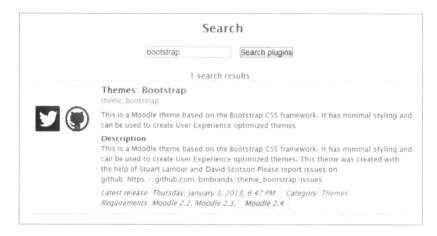

3. Click the **Bootstrap** link, and then on the next page select the **Download versions** tab. Select the correct version for your Moodle and download it.

4. This will download a ZIP file. Extract the contents of this ZIP file to your computer. It will contain a folder called `bootstrap`. This is your theme folder. Copy the `bootstrap` folder into your `<moodle site>/theme` folder.

5. Next, open your browser and log in to your Moodle as a site administrator. Moodle will detect the new theme and will immediately open the **Plugins check** screen. Click on the **Upgrade Moodle database now** button.

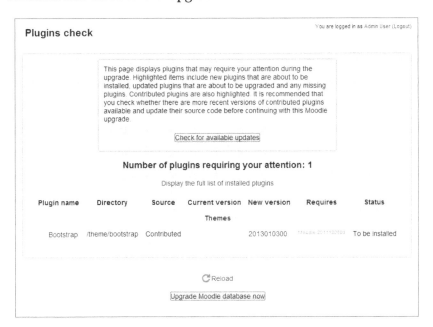

6. The theme will then be installed to Moodle and you will see a confirmation message. Click on the **Continue** button.

7. The next screen that displays is the Bootstrap theme settings page. This contains a number of fields as follows:

    ○   **Enable jquery**: This field enables a third-party JavaScript library called jQuery, and this checkbox should be selected unless you have a known reason not to use it.

    ○   **Enable Glyphicons**: This checkbox should be selected if you want to use the theme's own icons instead of the Moodle standard icons. We recommend that you leave this checkbox unselected for now, but come back later and try selecting the checkbox and see which you prefer.

    ○   **Logo URL**: This field should contain the full URL of your own site logo if you want to display it.

    ○   **Custom CSS**: This field is used add custom CSS to make minor changes to the theme without amending the code files. We recommend leaving this to proficient developers, and just ignore this field.

- ○ **Google analytics key**: This field should contain your Google Analytics key if you wish to set up your site with Google Analytics.

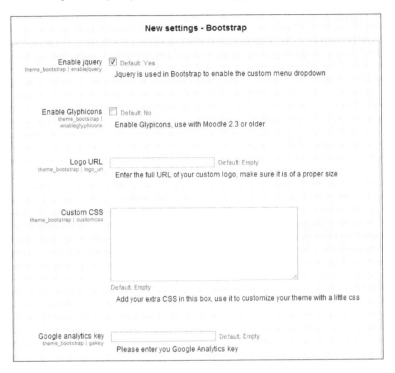

8. Click on **Save changes** at the bottom of the screen, and the theme setup is then complete.

The Bootstrap theme is now available on your Moodle site. The next task is to go into the Moodle **Theme selector** screen and set it up as the default site theme.

Carry out the following steps in order to set this up:

1. On the **ADMINISTRATION** block, navigate to **Site administration | Appearance | Themes | Theme selector**.

2. This will open up the **Theme selector** screen. There are four options listed under **Device type** that you can select: **Default**, **Legacy**, **Mobile**, and **Tablet**.

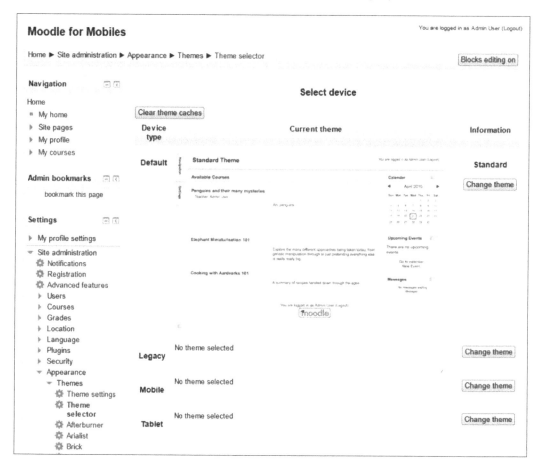

3. Click on the **Change theme** button next to the **Default device** type. On the next screen you are presented with a long list of themes, each with a screenshot. Scroll down to theme called **Bootstrap** and click on the **Use theme** button.

4. After clicking on the **Use theme** button, a confirmation screen is displayed. This will show the Bootstrap screenshot and some information about the theme. Click on **Continue**.

5. After clicking on **Continue** you will be taken back to the **Theme selector** screen, which will now display the newly selected **Bootstrap** theme next to the **Default** device type.

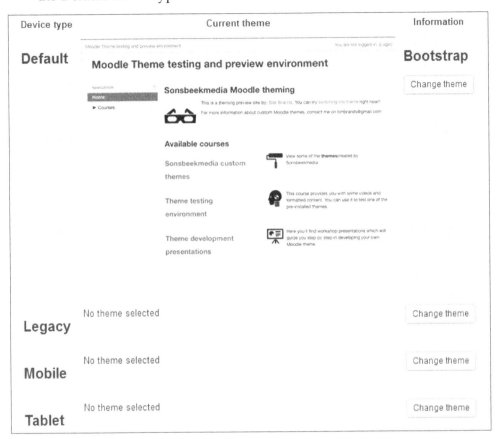

Setting up the Moodle Mobile app

Role: Site Administrator	**Version**: 2.4 and above

The Moodle Mobile app allows learners to:

- Select or capture an image and record audio or video from your mobile device and upload it into Moodle
- View their fellow course participants and associated contact information
- Use Moodle messaging if it is enabled
- Access to push notifications

The app will continue to evolve over time so new features will continually be added. Things to look out for include:

- Calendar sync
- Offline course browsing
- Offline posting in forums
- Offline grading

In order for the Moodle Mobile app to work there is one setup task that you must perform as a system administrator. That is to enable web services for mobile devices. Web services are simply a communication method that allows one software application to talk to another using a standard language, and they need to be enabled in the Moodle platform so that it can talk to the Moodle Mobile app.

Carry out the following steps in order to set up the Moodle Mobile app:

1. On the **ADMINISTRATION** block, navigate to **Site administration | Plugins | Web services | Mobile**.

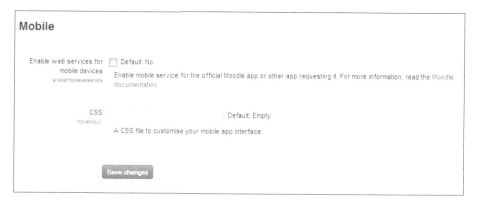

2. Select the checkbox labeled **Enable web services for mobile devices**, and then click on **Save changes**.
3. You will see a **Changes saved** notification towards the top of the screen, and you can then navigate away from this page.

That's it. Your Moodle is now ready to work with mobile apps.

Is Moodle Mobile an HTML5 app or a native app?

This is a confusing point for a lot of people. Moodle Mobile is a HTML5 web app, not a native app. There is a difference between the two types of app.

HTML5 web apps require an Internet connection, are hosted online instead of on the device, have limited use of hardware features such as the camera, and can cache data that can be useful for certain offline tasks (for example, the Google Docs HTML5 app allows offline document storage).

Native apps are fully accessible offline, can make full use of all hardware features, and generally have better performance. However, this is offset by the significant increase in development costs in maintaining multiple versions for different device types, such as Apple, Android, and BlackBerry.

Moodle Mobile is a HTML5 web app. It requires an Internet connection to perform optimally, but it performs some offline tasks; for example, if you upload a photo then this will be saved on the device cache and only uploaded to Moodle once an Internet connection is established.

Exploring the Moodle Mobile app

The Moodle Mobile app is straightforward to use and easy to understand.

When you open the Moodle Mobile app for the first time it asks you to enter the site URL, and your username and password. Once you have entered this information and clicked on **Add**, the app will add this site to its list of allowed sites.

You can go into the **Settings** page within the app at any point to add additional sites or to edit or remove existing sites.

Once you have added a site, you will enter the main menu page. This will contain a list of the courses that you are enrolled onto, and will reflect the same course list as on the menu page when you log in from a desktop computer.

Above the course list you have an **Upload** button. This will allow you to either upload image or audio files from your mobile device, or launch the mobile device's built-in camera and save the photo directly to the app.

Below the course list you have links to the **Website**, **Help**, and **Settings** pages. The **Website** link launches your standard Moodle site in the app's built-in browser, so this will only work with an Internet connection. Likewise, the **Help** link launches Moodle Docs online so also requires an Internet connection. **Settings** allows you to add, edit, or remove sites, manage sync settings, enable development settings, and report a bug.

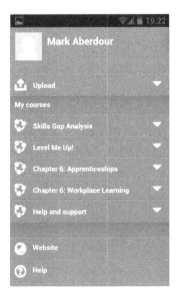

When you select a course from the menu page, you can either select **Contents** or **Participants**. When clicking on **Contents**, the first view is of the list of topics for the course. Clicking on a topic will reveal the activities and resources for that topic, or clicking on **Show all** will reveal every resource and activity within the topic titles, as shown in the following left-hand side screenshot.

Note that using this app requires some Internet connectivity. If you try viewing course contents with no Internet connection, such as in airplane mode, a connectivity warning message will be displayed and you will not be able to access the course contents.

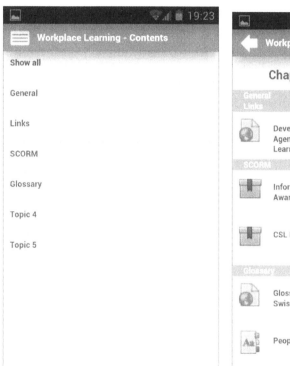 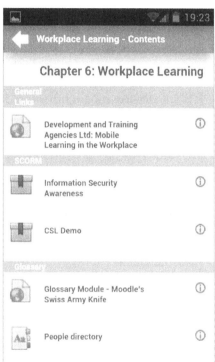

Third-party Moodle apps

There are a number of third-party apps available in the Android and Apple app stores that could work with your Moodle site, including one that works with Moodle 1.9:

- **mTouch**: This app is available for Apple iPhone, iPod Touch, and iPad only, and supports iOS 4.3 and above. It is for students' use only. It costs a couple of dollars to download and is under active development. It is available at http://www.pragmasql.com/moodletouch/home.aspx.

- **MoodleEZ (MoodleEasy)**: This app is available for iPad only, and supports iOS 4.3 and above. It is from the same makers as mTouch. It can be used used by students, teachers, and administrators. It costs a couple of dollars to download and is under active development. It is available at `https://itunes.apple.com/gb/app/moodlez/id449138373?mt=8`.

- **iActive** (previously mPage): This app is available for iPhone, iPod Touch, and iPad, and supports iOS 4.3 and above. It works with Moodle 1.9 and above, and seems quite fully featured in its scope, supporting blocks, files, assignments, forums, glossaries, quiz, SCORM, and more. It costs under a dollar to download and is under active development. It is available at `https://itunes.apple.com/gb/app/iactive/id577359069?mt=8`.

- **Droodle**: This app is is available for Android only and supports Android 2.2 and above. It is only for students, and centers around the ability of students to view their assignments and set up calendar reminders for assignments. It is free to download; however, it is *not* under active development. It is available at `https://play.google.com/store/apps/details?id=com.ivoid.droodle`.

- **mDroid**: This app is available for Android only and supports Android 2.0.1 and above. It is only for students, and gives access to all of the student's Moodle courses, files, and forums. It is free to download and is open source. It is under active development. It is available at `https://play.google.com/store/apps/details?id=in.co.praveenkumar`.

- **Moodle for Android**: This app is available for Android only, and supports Android 2.2 and above. It requires Moodle 2.2 or above. It is free to download and is open source. It is under active development. It is available at `https://play.google.com/store/apps/details?id=moodle.android.moodle`.

- **umm (Unofficial Moodle Mobile)**: This app is available via the Moodle plugins database, and supports Apple, Android, and BlackBerry devices. It is intended as a clone of the official but now unsupported Moodle Mobile iOS-only app that was launched by Moodle HQ in 2011 and subsequently pulled in 2012 before HQ embarked on a new HTML5 app direction. In fact, Moodle HQ hired the developer of this app, *Juan Leyva*, to build upon umm as the foundation of the next official Moodle Mobile app. It is available at `https://moodle.org/plugins/view.php?id=175`.

This list of apps above is current at the time of writing, but it is worth noting that some may drop away while other new ones arrive, so it is always worth going direct to your app store and searching on the term `Moodle` to see what is there at any given point in time. However, if you do this then please note that you will also see many results for Moodle apps built by individual education institutions, which will, of course, only be usable by students from that institution. These should be easy to identify as most have the institution's name in the app title, but not all do, so beware!

We are not going to cover the installation and set up of each of these, and the how-to guides in this book cover the official Moodle app only.

Add help and support guides by using the Book module

Role: Tutor	**Time**: 60 minutes and above	**Device**: Desktop

Success or failure in mobile learning can depend on strong use of the tools available for students. Not all students will be familiar with the full range of tools available in Moodle, so it is important to provide guidance for students on how to learn effectively online. Usability is the key, and students should be able to find the course easy to use. However, help also needs to be quick to find and easy to access.

A great way to distribute help and support materials is to set these up as a course page that is either available to guest users or that all users are automatically enrolled in:

The Book resource in Moodle is ideal for authoring the actual help and support resources. To create your help and support book resource, perform the following steps:

1. Click on the **Turn editing on** button, and then select **Add an activity or resource**, choosing **Book** from the drop-down menu.

2. The book settings screen includes the following fields:

    ° **Name**: This field contains some descriptive but short and simple text, such as `Help and support`

    ° **Description**: This field should contain some basic instructional text that will be displayed on the course page, and should be as short as possible

    ° **Display description on course page**: This checkbox should be selected in order that the brief instruction text is displayed on the course page itself

    ° **Chapter formatting**: This field will help you to select between numbers, bullets, indented, or no formatting

    ° **Custom titles**: This checkbox, if selected, will allow you to add a longer chapter title for display in the content area, while the default chapter title is displayed in the table of contents

3. Then click on **Save and return to course**.

4. Click on the book resource to enter it. The resource will be empty the first time it is viewed, in which case you will be asked to edit the first chapter.

5. In the first chapter, add a chapter title and your content into the fields provided, and then click on **Save changes**.

6. The next screen will display the chapter you just added. A **TABLE OF CONTENTS** block shows the chapters, while arrow icons on the right-hand side allow you to navigate through the book activity, or exit from it by using the up arrow.

7. On the **ADMINISTRATION** menu, navigate to **Book administration | Turn editing on**, and use the icons on the **TABLE OF CONTENTS** block to edit your book activity. From here you can perform any of the following tasks:

    ° Move the chapter up
    ° Move the chapter down
    ° Edit the chapter
    ° Delete the chapter
    ° Hide the chapter
    ° Add a new chapter

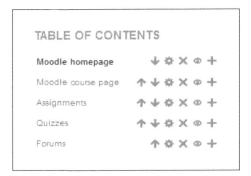

8. Continue adding new chapters until your help and support book activity is complete. On tablet and smartphone, the students will see something similar to the following screenshot. Note that on smartphone screens there is much less space available, so more scrolling is required to get down to the content area. On larger book resources the **TABLE OF CONTENTS** alone could fill a screen.

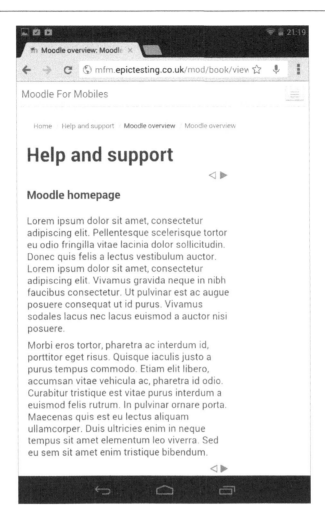

Add a link to help and support from the header bar

Role: Site Administrator	**Time**: 15 minutes and above	**Device**: Desktop

This handy tip will give mobile users quick access to support resources without having to scroll through the navigation block. Carry out the following steps:

1. Click on **ADMINISTRATION | Site administration | Appearance | Themes | Theme settings**.

2. Scroll down to the field **Custom menu items**. You can add menu items into the empty text box. Each line consists of some menu text, a link URL, and a tooltip title, separated by pipe characters.

3. So, to add a **Help and support** link you can add the text `Help and support|http://www.moodleformobiles.com/course/view.php?id=11|Help and support`, replacing the URL with that of your own course.

This will display a header bar throughout the site like the one shown in the following screenshot, which is shown using the Bootstrap theme.

The same view on a mobile device uses the native device menu, which is a small square icon in the top-right corner of the device screen, which when clicked on expands to show a collapsible menu, as shown in the following screenshots. This makes great use of screen space on a mobile device, and is a useful way to navigate to key sections of the site.

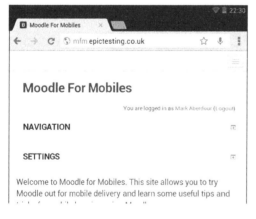
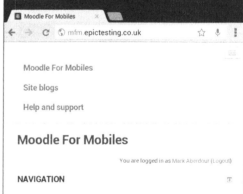

Summary

In this chapter we have provided you an overview of mobile themes that are available for you to use in your Moodle site, and looked at mobile apps that your students can download to access your Moodle site.

We looked at the official Clean theme that comes with Moodle, which delivers a layout that is appropriate to the screen resolution of the user's browser and offers a graceful solution to handling the wide variety of devices and screen sizes in the mobile device marketplace.

We also looked at the official Mobile Moodle HTML5 app, which is available for Android and Apple devices. This does not simply recreate Moodle on a mobile device, but concentrates on a number of specific tasks that learners are mostly likely to do on their mobile devices, such as image, video, and audio uploads, communicating with their fellow course attendees, and receiving notifications from Moodle.

We then looked briefly at the variety of third-party apps available on the Apple and Android app stores.

The instructions for the previous options should have got your Moodle into a position where you can start to deliver mobile learning. So let's now move on to next chapter where we will start our how-to guides for delivering specific mobile learning interventions.

3
Delivering Static Content to Mobiles

In this chapter we look at how to deliver static content from Moodle to mobile devices. By static content we mean content that does not involve the use of multimedia. We will deal with multimedia content in depth in *Chapter 4, Delivering Multimedia Content to Mobiles*.

Setting up file downloads

There are many different file types that you can make available in Moodle that are suited to mobile delivery, such as documents, slide presentations, spreadsheets, and images. The process for setting these up is essentially the same as for files viewed from a desktop computer, so there is no need to make one file available for desktop and another for mobile. Instead, there are some settings that you need to configure within the resource settings page to ensure that the file will work well on mobile devices.

To make a file available for mobile delivery, perform the following steps:

1. On your course page, click on the **Turn editing on** button. The editing icons are displayed:

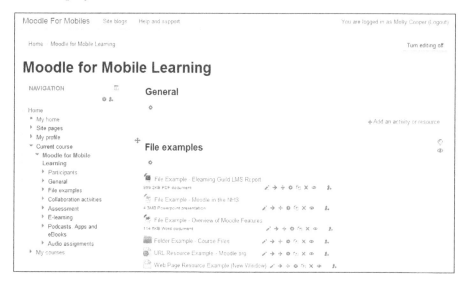

2. Click on **Add an activity or resource**, and then select **File** from the drop-down list.

3. On the next screen there are a number of fields to complete. Enter a filename and a description, and then click on **Add** to browse to your file and select it.

4. There are a number of display options to consider next, listed under **Appearance**, and it pays to select the right one as mobile devices will behave differently depending on what you select. Our recommendation is to use the **Open** option. This behaves naturally on all devices; on your desktop machine it will open in the browser and you can choose to save it if you wish; on your mobile it will download it, which is normal to users of mobiles devices. The added benefit for mobile users is that the document is then available for viewing offline and at a time suiting the learner. The full list of options is as follows:

   ° **Automatic**: On a mobile device Moodle tries to open this document as an embedded file first, and then asks you to click on the filename to download it, which adds an unnecessary click.

   ° **Embed**: Some mobile devices may not accept this method and will instead open a new page and ask you to click on a link to start the document download, again adding an unnecessary click.

   ° **Force download**: This will download the file immediately, which is technically fine, but the same behavior will also be forced on your desktop computer users, so this is not ideal.

   ° **Open**: This will download the file immediately for mobile users, and will attempt to open the file in the browser for desktop users. As this works well for all users, we recommend this method.

   ° **In pop-up**: Mobile devices cannot open multiple browser instances, so instead a new browser tab will open and the document will then automatically download, after which the tab will close, leaving you back on the course page. This adds an unnecessary tab opening and closing, which looks pretty awkward, so this option should be avoided.

5. Select the checkboxes **Show size** and **Show type**. This is important for mobile device users, and will automatically add the file type and size to the end of the filename so that users know what sort of file they are about to open and what size it is. Depending on their available bandwidth they may then make an informed choice about whether to open the file now or wait until they are on a better connection at a later time. Note that file type is also communicated via a small icon in front of the filename, but, this is not obvious in every case, so the **Show type** checkbox should still be selected.

6. Once the file is set up you can click on **Save and return to course**.

Learner view of file downloads

The learner view of a file resource is shown in the following screenshot, which was taken using a 7-inch Android tablet.

1. The learner clicks on a file such as a PDF file (the top-most link in this example), which is underlined once it is selected. A **Starting download** notification appears.

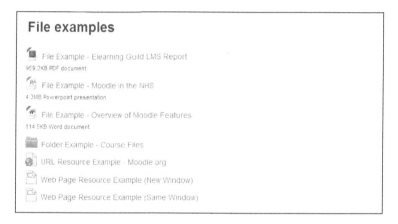

2. Once the download is complete, a small arrow appears in the top-left corner of the status bar at the top of the screen to indicate that the download is complete.

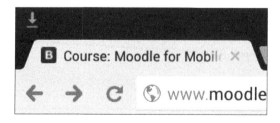

3. If the learner swipes down from the status bar to show the notification details, then the filename and time of download are displayed. Alternatively, the user can navigate to their **Downloads** area at any time and launch it from there.

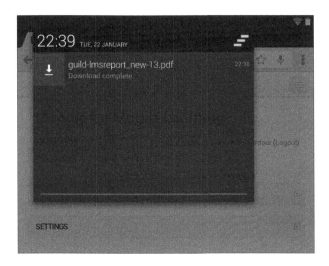

4. The user can then click directly on the filename to open it. In this example the file is a PDF document so opens in the device's PDF reader app.

A note about file types

There are a few points to mention regarding file type support within mobile devices. Typical file types you might want to include are PDF documents, Office documents (such as Microsoft Word and OpenOffice or LibreOffice Writer files), spreadsheets (such as Microsoft Excel and OpenOffice or LibreOffice Calc files), and slide presentations (such as Microsoft PowerPoint and OpenOffice or LibreOffice Impress files). You will need the appropriate viewing software on the mobile devices to view these, and not all devices may come bundled with them. If in any doubt, advise your students to install the appropriate apps to read the files that you are uploading, and only use common file formats. Examples include rollApp for viewing and editing OpenOffice files.

Setting up an eBook or App library

It's really simple to generate a list of eBook links to items on mobile app stores that your students can download.

1. On your course page, click on **Turn editing on**, and then in one of your topic areas, select **Add an activity or resource** and click on **Page**.

2. This opens the update page editor, where you can enter the page title, description, and content. The **Content** area is where you enter the details of your eBook and apps library.

3. In the following example we have added the eBook title, author, and description, and a link to the eBook in the main app stores for Android, Apple, and Kindle devices.

4. To find your own books, you will need to visit the app store that you wish to use. For example, the popular Amazon Kindle store and Google Play store can each be accessed via your web browser from a desktop computer. You can also download and install iTunes to access the iTunes Store if you wish to link to items from there. Performing this task from a desktop computer means that you are not limited to the store you can access. However, if you were to try accessing the iTunes catalogue from your Android device you would find this is not possible! If you access the Kindle and Google stores from your desktop computer's web browser, you can simply copy the address of the book page from your browser's address bar. In iTunes you can right-click on a book title and select **Copy Link**. In each case, the copied link can be pasted as a link into Moodle.

5. To paste your link, select the words in the page, such as **Android**, and then click on the **Insert/edit link** button on the bottom row of the toolbar. You can roll your mouse cursor over the buttons to reveal a tooltip containing the button name, if needed.

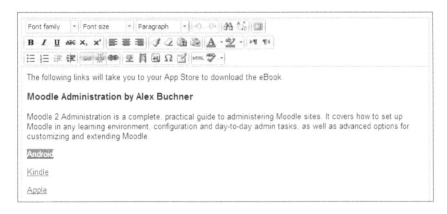

6. In the **Insert/edit link** dialog box, you can then paste the URL into the **Link URL** field. Set the **Target** and **Title** fields as needed, and click on **Update**. There is no need to change any other fields unless you have specific reason to.

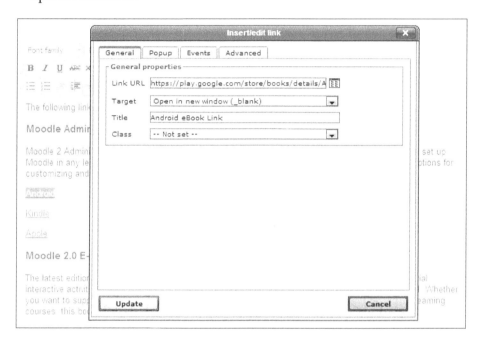

7. Click on **Update** and then, on the settings screen, click on **Save and display** to view your page.

Learner view of a library

The tablet view shown in the following screenshot displays most of the eBook library page. Bear in mind the amount of scrolling that may be required on small device browsers, so limit the amount of text to the minimum possible.

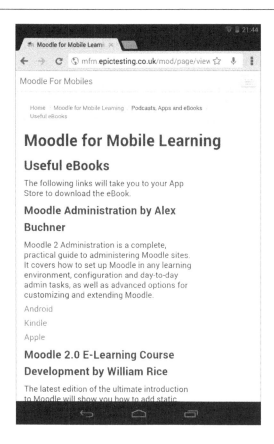

Using QR codes in courses

Role: Student	**Time**: 30 minutes and above	**Device**: Smartphone or Tablet

A QR code is an image that can be scanned by a QR code reader. This is conceptually similar to a bar code but can be scanned in by smartphones, which will convert the QR code to a URL and launch it in the phone's browser.

The intention is to link physical objects to web pages, and despite being invented for industrial use, they are now commonly seen in magazines and billboard advertisements, and have many uses in education.

- QR codes are used for QR code treasure hunts that require students to locate and scan QR codes. Each web page that the QR code links to will contain one part of the answer to the exercise, and after collecting all the data the students can complete a quiz.

- Printed materials can include QR codes for students to scan and download the handout to their mobile devices.

- QR handouts can include links to further reading that will automatically open on students' mobile devices.

- Printed materials and posters can include QR codes to subscribe to department or lecturer blog RSS feeds, which can be quickly subscribed to by using an RSS aggregator on a mobile phone.

- Specific activities within printed workbooks can include QR codes to link directly to specific forums on the VLE.

- You can provide a QR code to link to extension activities on a class assignment handout.

- You can attach QR codes to workstations and lab equipment with links to usage instructions and supplemental information.

There are many online tools that will generate QR codes for you. `http://www.delivr.com/` comes highly recommended.

Quick case study – University of Bath

The e-learning team at University of Bath created a small customization for their Moodle that automatically puts a QR code for the Moodle page onto any page that was printed out from Moodle. This allowed students to simply scan the QR code to link to the page, eliminating any URL copying errors. Examples of scenarios where this might be used include printing out quiz questions, database submissions, wiki pages, and more.

Building a multidevice SCORM resource

Role: Tutor	**Time**: 1 day and above	**Device**: Desktop

E-learning SCORM packages have been the dominant form of online learning in the corporate world since the 1990s, although they are less widely used in the education sector. SCORM stands for **Sharable Content Object Reference Model** and is a standard that enables content developers to create a single e-learning course with the confidence that it will work with all SCORM-compliant learning management systems.

At least that's the theory. In practice, there are hundreds of authoring tools and learning management systems in the marketplace, and not all of them have implemented SCORM in the same manner so it hasn't achieved the true interoperability that was hoped for, but it has certainly gone a long way towards it.

There are many tools available for building SCORM resources, and these are known as authoring tools. These come in the form of cloud-based tools (such as GoMo Learning), desktop applications (such as Articulate and Captivate), and open source tools (such as Xerte Online Toolkits).

There are many considerations to make when selecting a SCORM authoring tool for mobile learning. For example, if you want to develop once and deliver to multiple devices, you need a tool that can do this. If a vendor claims to deliver mobile output, check that they are referring to smartphones as well as tablets and that they support Android and BlackBerry as well as Apple devices.

You will also need to have peace of mind that the content displayed on smartphones provides a comparable learning experience to the tablet or desktop versions, and that it adapts the user interactions appropriately rather than simply scaling down the tablet version for the smaller smartphone screen.

Multidevice SCORM authoring involves new ways of thinking about content creation. *Imogen Casebourne*, Head of Learning Design at Epic advises:

> *"If you anticipate a 50/50 PC/smartphone split for a statutory and mandatory e-learning course, go for bite-size topics and a flat navigation structure so the course won't be too onerous for learners on phones. On the other hand, if the majority of learners will take the course from a PC and only occasionally dip into it via a smartphone, then this will be less of a consideration."*

Do your research well and find out what has been done before, and learn lessons from those who have already tried.

Ultimately, you are looking to output something like the course shown in the following screenshot, which was built in GoMo Learning. On the tablet version, when the graphic is selected on the right-hand column, supporting information slides in from the left. However, on the smartphone, not only does the product perform in a responsive manner by scaling down to a single column, but the actual user interactions change too so that when the user selects the same hot graphic, the supporting information pops up over the text, instead of sliding in.

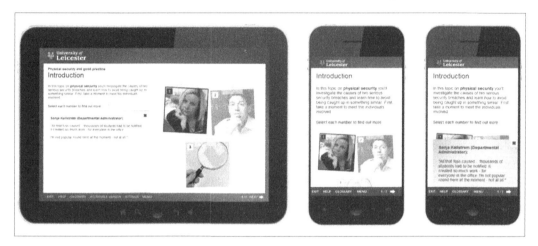

Adding a multidevice SCORM resource into Moodle

Role: Tutor	**Time**: 15 minutes and above	**Device**: Desktop

So, you've built or purchased a multidevice SCORM resource. What do you do with it now in order to get it working nicely in your multidevice Moodle?

Moodle's SCORM activity accepts SCORM 1.2 or AICC packages, and there is also the IMS Content Package resource type, all of which can be added into a Moodle course.

IMS Content Package and **SCORM** are both e-learning packaging standards. However, IMS is principally for presentational content while SCORM allows question interactions with tracking of answers and a grade at the end. For this reason, in Moodle you will find IMS Content Package under **Resources** and SCORM under **Activities**. It is worth noting that a Moodle **Book** activity can be exported as an IMS Content Package and then reused in other systems.

To add a SCORM activity into Moodle, perform the following steps:

1. Click on **Add an activity or resource** and select **SCORM package**.

2. On the **Adding a new SCORM package** screen there are a number of important fields to complete in order to set the activity up for an optimal mobile experience.

In the **General** and **Package** field groups we have some of the usual fields, including:

- **Name**: The name value should be kept fairly short so that it displays well on a small screen

- **Description**: The description entered will appear on the launch page or on the course page if you select **Display description on course page**

- **Package file**: This field will allow browse to your SCORM ZIP package and upload it, or drag it in if your browser supports dragging and dropping files

In the **Appearance** group we have a number of important fields, including:

° The **Display package** drop-down list allows you to select **New window** or **Current window**. **New window** will open a new browser window to display the SCORM e-learning, which can be useful if you want the e-learning to go full screen and provide a maximum engagement to the learner, who is then less likely to be distracted by events in other windows they may have open.

° Click on **Show more...** to reveal some more fields. The screen **Width** and **Height** fields are only enabled if **New window** is selected in the **Display package** drop-down list. Here you can specify the window dimensions of the new window the e-learning will launch in, for example, **1024** x **768**. The **Options** values are only enabled if **New window** is selected. This displays a list of checkboxes for controlling the browser behavior, such as allowing the window to be resized and scrolled, and showing various browser elements such as the location bar, address bar, menu bar, toolbar, and status bar. Generally speaking, the more browser elements you remove the more space there is to display the e-learning content, and the fewer distractions there are for the learner.

° The **Student skip content structure page** drop-down list should be set to **Always** if the SCORM package only contains one learning object. Sometimes SCORM packages are built containing multiple learning objects, in which case the content structure page can be a useful navigational aid. However, SCORMs with multiple learning objects are fairly uncommon.

° The **Disable preview mode** drop-down list will hide the preview button, which can be used by learners if they wish to browse an activity before attempting it. This would normally be set to **Yes** as there is very little need for this feature in workplace learning environments.

° The **Display course structure on entry page** drop-down list will display a table of contents on the SCORM entry page. By way of some background, the native behavior—when a learner clicks on a SCORM link—is to first display an entry page that contains details about the SCORM activity, the attempts taken so far, and a launch button to actually open the SCORM activity. However, given that most SCORM modules actually have their own internal navigation and start menu, it is unnecessary to display a course structure on the entry page.

- ° The **Display course structure in player** drop-down list provides options for how the course structure can be displayed once the SCORM activity has opened in Moodle's SCORM player, after the user has clicked on the **Enter** button on the SCORM entry page. This can be set to **Disabled**, **In a dropdown menu**, **Hidden**, or **To the side**. As noted previously, most SCORM modules have their own internal navigation and start menu, in which case we do not need to have the course structure displayed in the player at all, so we would select **Disabled** in this menu.

- ° The **Display attempt status** drop-down list will allow you to show attempt statuses on either the SCORM entry page, and/or on the **COURSE OVERVIEW** block in **My home**, or not at all.

In the **Grade** group we have fields including the following:

- ° The **Grading method** drop-down list defines how the grade for a single attempt of the activity is determined. This could be one of the following options: **Learning objects** (number of completed or passed learning objects), **Highest grade** (highest score obtained from all of the passed learning objects), **Average grade** (the mean of all scores obtained), or **Sum grade** (the sum of all of the scores obtained). This field assumes two things: that the SCORM module is graded and that it contains multiple learning objects. However, SCORM modules are often presentational in nature and do not have an assessment in them, in which case they would pass no grade back to the system at all, only a completion status. Also, as discussed earlier, most SCORM modules only contain a single learning object, in which case they would only pass a single grade and it does not matter which of these options is selected.

In the **Attempts management** group we have fields including the following:

- ° The **Number of attempts** drop-down list allows you to control how many times learners are able to access the SCORM activity (usually this will be set to **Unlimited**).

- ° The **Attempts grading** drop-down list controls how the score is recorded in the gradebook when multiple attempts are allowed. This can be set to:
  - **Highest attempt**: This would allow the learner to keep improving their grade over time
  - **Average attempts**: This will calculate the average grade from all attempts
  - **First attempt**: This will only record the grade from the first attempt and allow further ungraded attempts
  - **Last completed attempt**: This will pass the grade from the most recent attempt into the gradebook
- ° The **Force new attempt** drop-down list will log a new attempt every time the SCORM module is accessed. This would normally be set to **Yes** so that each attempt is tracked properly.
- ° The **Lock after final attempt** drop-down list can be used lock access to the SCORM after the number of attempts has been met. This would normally be set to **No**.

In the **Compatibility settings** group we have fields including:

- ° The **Force completed** drop-down list should be set to **Yes** if there are known issues with SCORM 1.2 packages not setting the completion status correctly. This will force the status of the current attempt to show **Completed**. This would normally be set to **No**.
- ° The **Auto-continue** drop-down list will enable sequential learning objects within a SCORM package to be launched automatically, instead of requiring the user to click on a **Continue** button.

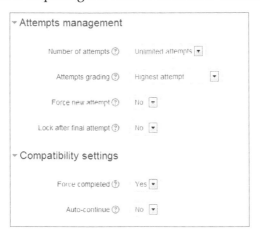

3. Click on **Save and return to course** at the bottom of the settings page.

Case study – using a multidevice SCORM resource for information security awareness training

Information security training is a vital requirement for many organizations. Delivering face-to-face training to staff presents considerable logistical challenges, as well as being costly. In universities this is a particular concern because a great deal of personal data is gathered and stored during academic research projects. To cater for this important staff training need, a consortium of five universities—Leicester, Leeds, Cranfield, Southampton, and Imperial College London—and multidevice e-learning specialists Epic came together to develop an **Information Security Awareness Learning Suite**, or "**Infosec**".

Narrative-based learning scenarios were developed using Epic's GoMo Learning multidevice authoring tool. This cloud-based tool enabled each university to take the template Infosec courses and customize them with local examples targeted to their own audience. The modules are fully accessible and are deployed on all major mobile platforms including Apple iPhones/iPads, Android smartphones and tablets, and BlackBerry devices. This multidevice approach means that the modules can be accessed by the widest possible audience.

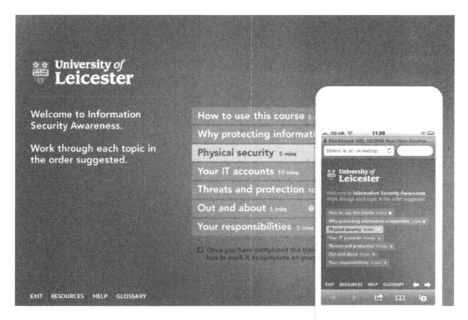

This SCORM resource was tested specifically with Moodle and Blackboard, and it is now in use in many other further education institutions, including Exeter, Derby, Sheffield, East Anglia, and New College Durham, for their own staff training. In February 2012, the Information Security Awareness Learning Suite was awarded the 2011 UCISA-Eduserve Award for Excellence, which seeks to recognize and highlight levels of excellence and best practice demonstrated by UCISA members within the UK higher and further education sectors.

Using cohorts to deliver performance-support resources

Role: Tutor	**Time**: 15 minutes and above	**Device**: Desktop

Mobile employees need quick access to performance-support resources, and the LMS is the perfect place from which to deliver these. Increasingly, LMS administrators are thinking beyond lengthy courses and more in terms of providing support materials to employees at the point of need. This is often referred to as "just-in-time" learning, or "performance support" and comes in many guises, although the principle is that employees need quick access to materials relevant to their job, that they can consume during their daily workflow, rather than having to be relocated to a training room and away from their work, with all of the lost productivity that brings with it.

Helpfully, Moodle has a feature that enables us to deliver materials related to employees' job roles. **Cohorts** are a course enrolment method for batch enrolling users onto multiple courses, and they take a lot of the headache out of course enrolment.

An example scenario would be a multinational organization using cohorts for broad job families, such as Finance, Finance-UK, and Finance-Germany. An employee joining the Finance team in Germany would be added to the general Finance cohort and therefore would automatically be enrolled on any courses assigned to that cohort, but can also be added to Finance-Germany cohort and be enrolled to any courses that are unique to that country, for example, there are often regulatory law courses specific to individual countries. As we have seen, a Moodle course can be made up purely of resources if we wish to set it up that way, so a page of performance-support resources or "job aids" could easily be set up as a course, and could provide a quick go-to resource for employees looking for resources and document templates relevant to their job, for example, German financial regulations.

To set up a cohort, perform the following steps:

1. Click on **ADMINISTRATION | Site administration | Users | Accounts | Cohorts**.

2. On the **System: available cohorts** screen, click on **Add**.

3. On the **Add new cohort** screen there are just four fields to fill in: **Name**, **Context** (which can be system-wide or within a named category), **Cohort ID** (which can be used during bulk user imports from a CSV file), and **Description** (which is just used for administrative purposes; the employee will not see this).

4. lick on **Save changes**.

5. On the **System: available cohorts** screen you will now see your updated list of cohorts:

6. Before we add users, we need to assign courses to the cohorts. Enter a course that you wish to assign to a particular cohort, and then in the **ADMINISTRATION** block, choose **Course administration | Users | Enrolment methods**.

7. This will launch the **Enrolment methods** page, where you need to tell Moodle that you wish to allow cohorts to be assigned to this course. To do this, in the **Add method** drop-down box, select **Cohort sync**.

8. The **Cohort sync** page will then open and you will see five fields, including:

   ° **Cohort**: This is the only required field, and is where you select from the list of available cohorts.

   ° **Assign role**: This allows you to assign a role within the current course for all users enrolled via this cohort.

  ° **Add to group**: This allows you to assign users that are added to the course from this cohort to a specific course group.

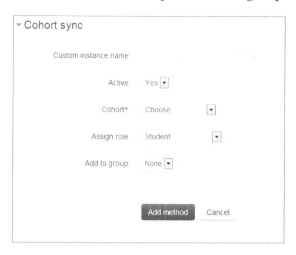

9. Click on **Add method** when you have specified all required information.

10. You will now be back at the **Enrolment methods** page, which has been updated with the details of the new cohort sync method, as shown in the following screenshot:

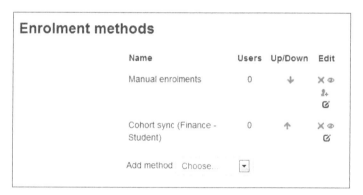

11. Currently there are no members of the cohorts, so the **Cohort size** value is **0**. To add users into your cohort, click on **ADMINISTRATION | Site administration | Users | Accounts | Cohorts**.

12. On the **System: available cohorts** screen you can now enroll users into your cohorts.

13. In the **Edit** column you will see three icons, which represent Delete, Edit, and Members.

14. Click on the Members icon and the `Cohort 'Name' members` page, where `'Name'` is the name of the cohort you selected. On the right -hand side of this screen are **Potential users** that you can add to the cohort. Select one or more users, then click on the **Add** button to add them to the **Current users** box on the left. Then click on the **Back to cohorts** button at the bottom of the screen.

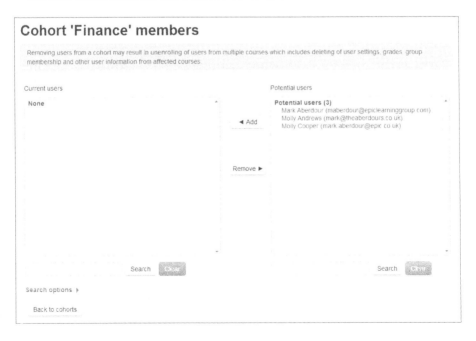

15. You will now see the **Cohort size** value has been incremented by the number of users that you just added.

Name	Cohort ID	Description	Cohort size	Source	Edit
Finance	finance	Cohort for ALL finance employees across the company.	3	Created manually	✕ ⚙ 👤

16. Continue setting up courses to job-related cohorts as you see fit. When one of the users belonging to that cohort logs in to Moodle, they will see all of the courses related to their job role on their course menu.

Naming your course something like "UK Finance job aids" will ensure that employees can easily find this on their menu when they need it, ensuring that important job-based resources are only one-click away.

Using a glossary for staff induction

Role: Tutor   **Time**: 30 minutes and above   **Device**: Desktop

One of the most common forms of online learning in the workplace is staff induction, also often referred to as onboarding or orientation. This is often the first experience that employees will have of online learning so it's important that they get a good impression. For this reason many organizations will invest heavily in a flagship e-learning course and still achieve good return on investment due to the money saved on sending people for face-to-face induction days. It's not uncommon for global enterprises to fly staff internationally to attend induction days, so the savings from delivering this via e-learning can be quite staggering. An induction course can be split across multiple activities, such as pre-induction content, quizzes, and forums.

One useful activity type is **Glossary**, which enables participants to create and maintain a list of definitions, or to collect and organize resources or information, as we will do here. Files can be attached to glossary entries, and the attached images are displayed in the entry. Entries can be searched or browsed alphabetically or by category, date, or author. Entries can be automatically approved, or can require approval by a teacher before they are viewable by everyone.

One potential use of **Glossary** is for a staff directory. To set up a glossary, perform the following steps:

1. Click on **Add an activity or resource**, and then select **Glossary**.

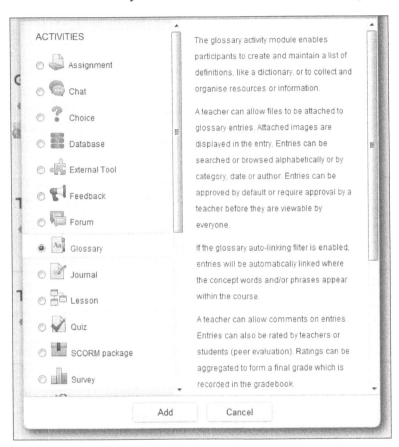

2. On the **Adding a new Glossary** screen there are a number of important fields to complete. Under **General** you will find the following fields:

    ° The **Is this glossary global?** checkbox should be selected if you want to link to the glossary throughout the site, which we would not necessarily want to do for an induction course.

    ° The **Glossary type** drop-down list has two options: **Main glossary** and **Secondary glossary**. A main glossary can import entries from secondary glossaries, but there can only be one main glossary in a course. If glossary entry import is not required, all glossaries in the course can be secondary glossaries, so that this the option we shall use in our example.

Under **Entries** you will find the following fields:

- ° The **Always allow editing** field allows entries to be edited by the author at any time. If set to **No**, users will have a configured editing time (usually 30 minutes).

- ° The **Duplicate entries allowed** drop-down list, when enabled, will allow duplicate entries of the same name.

- ° The **Allow comments on entries** drop-down list allows comments to be added to glossary entries.

- ° The **Automatically link glossary entries** drop-down list allows the entries to be linked whenever the concept words or phrases are used throughout the course. If the global glossary setting is enabled, this can be used site-wide.

- ° The **Approved by default** drop-down list can be set to **Yes** or **No** depending on whether or not you want teachers to approve submitted glossary entries.

Under **Appearance** you will find the following fields:

- ° The **Display format** drop-down list can be set to one of the following seven formats:

  - **Simple, dictionary style**: No authors are displayed, and attachments are shown as links.

  - **Continuous without author**: Entries are displayed one after another without any separation, apart from the editing icons.

  - **Full with author**: A forum-like display format showing the author's data, and with attachments shown as links.

  - **Full without author**: A forum-like display format without authors, and with attachments shown as links. This is most suitable for a staff directory as it does not include the author's name on each entry, and allows the user to click on the image attachment to view a photo.

  - **Encyclopedia**: As for **Full with author** but attached images are shown inline. This is suitable for a staff directory; however, it includes the author's name on each entry.

  - **Entry list**: Concepts are listed as links.

  - **FAQ**: The words **QUESTION** and **ANSWER** are appended to the concept and definition respectively.

- ◦ The **Approval display format** drop-down list allows the format to be changed once the entry is approved.
- ◦ The **Show 'Special' link** drop-down list allows users to browse the glossary by using special characters such as @ and #.
- ◦ The **Show alphabet** drop-down list will display the letters of the alphabet for users to browse the glossary by.
- ◦ The **Show 'ALL' link** drop-down list allows participants to display all entries on a single page.
- ◦ The **Allow print view** drop-down list allows users to print out glossary entries.

3. Click on **Save and display** to enter the new glossary activity.
4. This will display an empty glossary activity.

5. Click on **Add a new entry** to display the new entry form. There are just four fields on this screen:
   - ◦ **Concept**: This is the actual glossary term. In the case of a people directory, we will add the person's name here.
   - ◦ **Definition**: This goes with the concept name, so in our case we will add the person's description.
   - ◦ **Keywords**: This can be associated with an entry, and will be linked from content pages if auto-linking is enabled.

       ° **Attachment**: This allows you to add one of more files to an entry. In the case of our people directory example, we shall add a photo of the person here.

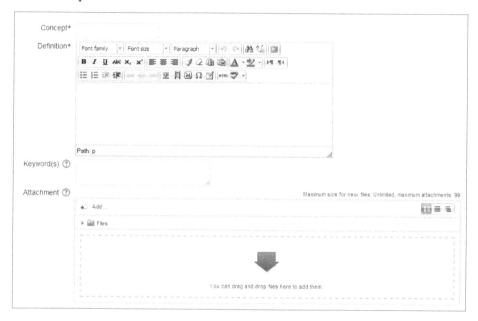

6. Click on **Save changes**.

This will be displayed on a mobile device as follows:

In this example we have used the **Full without author** display format. This shows the entries organized alphabetically, and has an **ALL** option to view them all on one page. Any attachments are displayed as links to click on.

If we switch to the **Encyclopedia** view, the photo is displayed inline, which works well for a **People directory**. However, this view also displays the author name and photo, which is less useful for something like a **People directory**. However, this could be hidden by a CSS developer if necessary, in which case it would be the preferable view for **People directory**.

Using a Glossary for best practice resource collection

Role: Tutor	**Time**: 15 minutes and above	**Device**: Desktop

The other obvious use for the glossary module is a **Frequently Asked Questions** area for new starters. As you may have noticed, the glossary activity has a number of display formats, one of which is **Frequently Asked Questions**. This is exactly the sort of thing that a new starter may need access to on a mobile device as they are finding their way around a new building, or viewing on the bus on their journey to work.

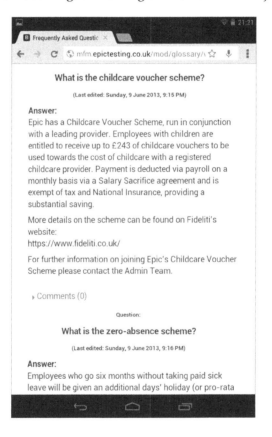

To set up **New Starters FAQ**, add a **Glossary** activity in the same manner as described previously, but this time select **FAQ** for **Display Format**. When you add a new entry the form is identical to the one shown in the previous section; however, when viewed by the user the entries are displayed in a **Question** and **Answer** format, as shown in the previous screenshot.

Using levels to engage new starters

Role: Tutor	**Time**: 15 minutes and above	**Device**: Desktop

There are many techniques for engaging learners during completion of a course, and a very simple technique that can be used in Moodle is to use a course structure based on games. This is useful for mobile learning as you only have short periods of your user's time and need all of the engagement tools that you can think of to keep your learners using the site.

This technique uses a standard **Topics format** course, but sets up each topic to be revealed in turn based on some completion criteria, such as an end of topic assessment. On first entry to the course **Level 1** is revealed, and further levels are only revealed as the user progresses.

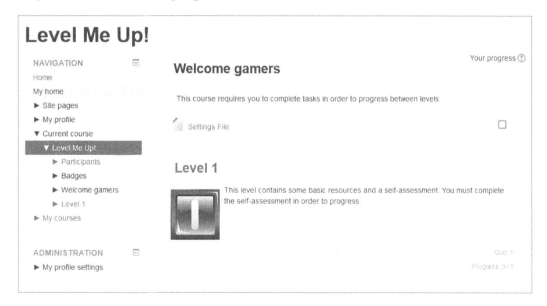

To set up a course based on games using levels, perform the following steps:

1. Click on **Course administration | Edit settings**.
2. Under **General**, select **Topics format** as the value for **Format**.
3. Under formatting options for **Topics format** select the following:
    - **Number of sections**: Here we select **3**, as we are setting up three levels, but you can choose whatever number you wish.

- ○ **Hidden sections**: Here we select **Hidden sections are completely invisible**. This will allow levels to be automatically "revealed" when the user "levels up".

- ○ **Course layout**: Here we select **Show one section per page**. This allows each level to have its own distinct identity and set of resources.

4. Under **Student progress**, select **Enabled, control via completion and activity settings** for **Completion tracking**.

This will set up your course settings correctly. You now need to set up the activities in each section. On the first entry to the course, the **Level 1** title and summary field will be shown automatically (shown in the following left-hand side screenshot) and the title can be clicked on to enter the actual level (shown in the following right-hand side screenshot). In this example we have just added a single assessment to illustrate the concept of leveling up; however, in this level, or section, you would add all of your resources and activities as in any normal Moodle course. In this case, the user has to complete an assessment in order to progress to **Level 2**.

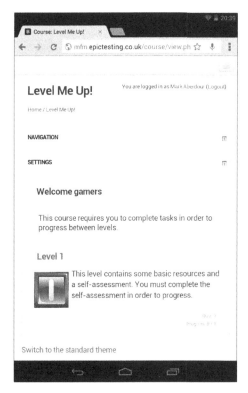 

In order to reveal **Level 2** automatically, click on **Summary Settings** of Level 2, shown as a cog icon under the summary field.

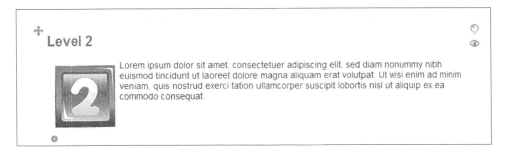

In the summary settings page, under **Restrict access | Grade condition**, add a minimum grade that will unlock **Level 2**. Also, under **Before section can be accessed**, select **Hide section entirely**, bearing in mind that you could also select to keep the section visible but grayed out if you wish by selecting the alternative option in this field.

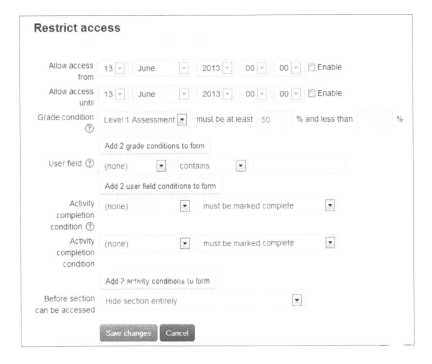

Now when a user completes the assessment and scores over 50 percent, upon going back to the course page, they will see **Level 2** has been revealed, as shown in the following left-hand side screenshot. It is worth noting that you could give a congratulatory "leveling up" message in the quiz pass feedback too.

When the level title is clicked on, the user will enter the actual level (shown in the following right-hand side screenshot).

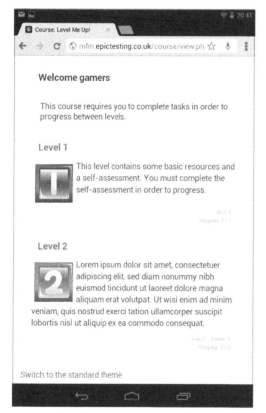 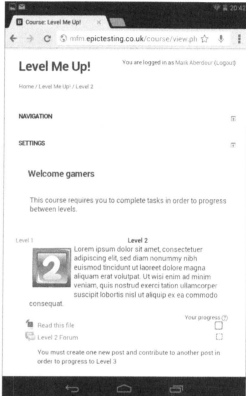

In order to reveal **Level 3** automatically, we are going to select a different completion setting. Leveling up is one form of increasing user engagement, however activity completion settings can also be used to encourage users to participate in collaborative activities that themselves have the potential to engage the user in a course more than a simple presentational piece of e-learning.

Therefore, in order to progress to **Level 3**, we are not going to put the user through an assessment, but this time will request that the user creates a new forum post, and replies to another forum post, in order to level up.

Firstly we will need to set up the activity completion settings for the **Forum** activity. To do this, enter the **Forum** settings page, and under **Activity completion**, select the checkboxes next to **Require discussions** and **Require replies**, leaving the value of each at **1**.

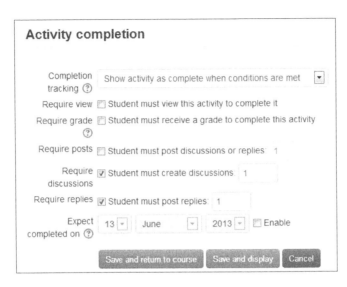

Of course, you can amend these settings to force a different number of posts or replies if you wish.

Next, click on **Summary Settings** of **Level 3**, which is shown as a cog icon under the summary field.

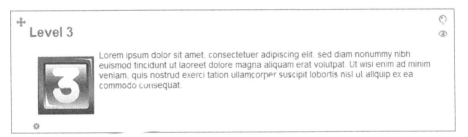

In the summary settings page, under **Restrict access | Activity completion condition**, select the **Forum** activity that you want users to participate in on the left, and select **must be marked complete** on the right, which will unlock **Level 3**.

Also, under **Before section can be accessed**, select **Hide section entirely**, bearing in mind that you could also select to keep the section visible but grayed out if you wish, by selecting the alternative option in this field.

Now when a user posts a forum post and replies to one post, when they return to the course page, they will see that **Level 3** has been revealed, as shown in the following left-hand side screenshot. When the level title is clicked on, the user will enter the actual level (shown in the following right-hand side screenshot).

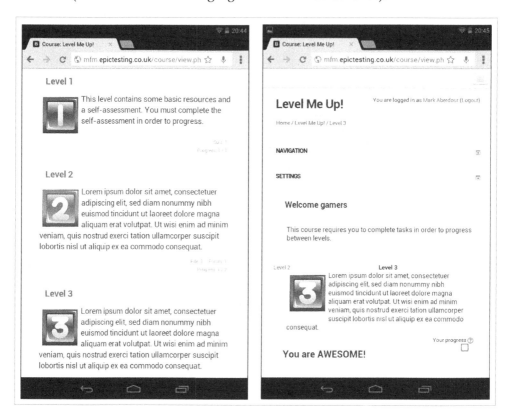

Summary

In this chapter we have provided you with ideas for delivering content to mobile devices from your Moodle site. We focused on file resources, links to eBook and App libraries, using QR codes, SCORM resources, and the glossary activity. We also looked at a use of the cohorts features for delivering performance-support resources that are particularly relevant for mobile delivery, and the use of levels based on games to engage your mobile learners.

In this chapter we only looked at what we call static content, such as files and web pages. But there is, of course, a whole other world of content commonly termed "multimedia" that may use audio, video, and animation. The next chapter looks at multimedia content in more depth.

4
Delivering Multimedia Content to Mobiles

In this chapter, we look at how to deliver multimedia content from Moodle to mobile devices.

Setting up a podcast

Audio can be a useful addition to your course, either to support students who are poor readers, or to support a specific topic or subject, such as language learning, telephone skills, and tone of voice topics, all of which are unlikely to be completely effective without some audio.

Audio is also useful for the 5 to 10 percent of the population who have some form of dyslexia. Although this may be mild in many cases, it's another barrier to learning for those who may find it difficult to learn through text-heavy content.

Do use audio wisely, though. An abundance of audio can slow down an online learning experience to an intolerable pace for fast readers who simply prefer text. The trick is in achieving the right balance.

There are a number of advantages and disadvantages to podcasting. The following list should help you decide if this is right for your course:

Advantages:

- Most learners can hear
- Many learners have problems with reading
- Good for learners with visual impairments

- Good for learners with low levels of literacy or with dyslexia
- Good for learners for whom English is a second language
- Some content needs sound to be effective; for example, language learning

Disadvantages:

- Learners are not able to listen at their own pace
- Needs good skills and tools to produce and update
- Depending on production qualities, can be moderately expensive
- Requires specific plugins and hardware (for example, headphones)
- Localization is difficult and expensive

There are podcasting modules for Moodle, but first we shall set up a podcast using a Moodle forum with an RSS feed that can be picked up in iTunes or other podcasting tools. To do this perform the following steps:

1. Go to **ADMINISTRATION | Site administration | Advanced features**. Scroll down to the **Enable RSS feeds** checkbox and select it, and then click on **Save changes** at the bottom of the screen.

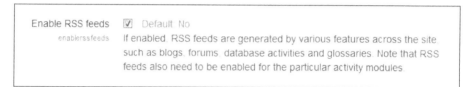

2. Go to **ADMINISTRATION | Site administration | Plugins | Activity modules | Forum**. Scroll down to the **Enable RSS feeds** drop-down box and select **Yes**, and then click on **Save changes** at the bottom of the screen.

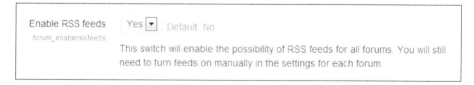

3. Then in your course page, click on **Turn editing on** and then click on **Add an activity or resource**.

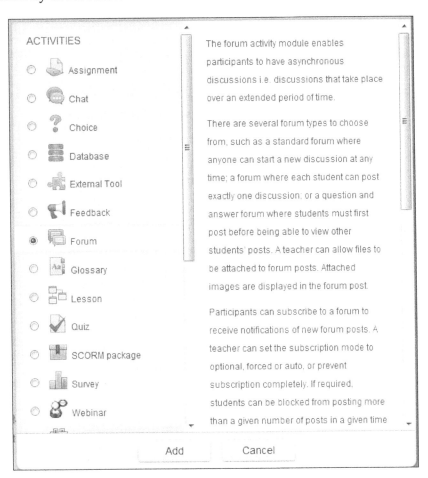

4. In the forum settings, there will now be an RSS section. Select **Posts** in the **RSS feed for this activity** drop-down box, and select the number of recent articles you want to display in the podcast feed, in the **Number of RSS recent articles** drop-down box.

5. In the forum settings, there will is also an **Attachments and word count** section. In the **Maximum attachment size** field, select an appropriate value. If in doubt, choose the highest attachment size allowed.

6. All other fields should be fine to leave with their default settings. Note that there are a set of **Ratings** field, should you wish learners to be able to rate your podcasts.

7. Click on **Save and return to course** at the bottom of the page.

8. Enter the forum and click on **Add a new discussion topic**.

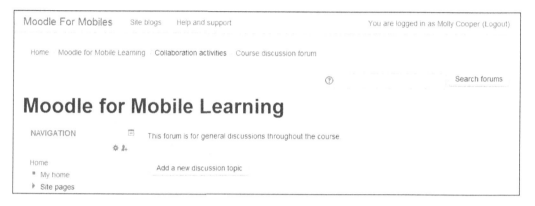

9. Specify your subject, message (description of podcast), and attach the MP3 file for your podcast. Then click on **Post to forum**.

Learner view of podcasts

The learner view of a podcast resource is shown in the following screenshot (taken using a 7-inch Android tablet):

1. On your course page, navigate to the podcast forum activity.

2. Expand the **SETTINGS** block if it is not already expanded.

3. Under **Forum administration**, click on the **RSS feed of posts** link.

4. This will open the RSS URL, which can be copied into iTunes or similar software to subscribe to the podcast. Alternatively, it may open a podcasting app on the mobile device automatically if such an app has been installed.

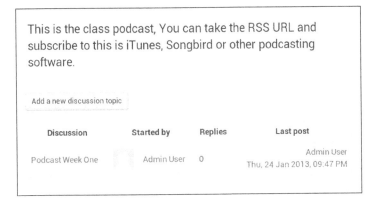

This is the class podcast, You can take the RSS URL and
subscribe to this is iTunes, Songbird or other podcasting
software.

Add a new discussion topic

Discussion	Started by	Replies	Last post
Podcast Week One	Admin User	0	Admin User Thu, 24 Jan 2013, 09:47 PM

Audio add-on

There are audio add-ons for Moodle that embed an audio recorder into Moodle.
Because these are submitted to the Moodle community by contributing developers,
they should always be thoroughly tested before using in a live environment.
Features typically offered by audio add-ons include:

- **Online audio recording**: This is an assignment type that allows students
  to record an audio clip from their microphone and upload it into Moodle
  as an MP3

- **YouTube submission**: This is an assignment type that allows students to
  record video clips and upload them to YouTube, and make them accessible
  from within the Moodle assignment activity

- **Record audio**: This allows teachers to record audio from their microphone
  and upload this into Moodle as a file for playing back within a course

- **Media capture**: This adds a media file repository with audio recorder,
  for teachers to record audio files for insertion into their courses

Providing audio instructions

Teachers can use a voice recorder on their mobile device to record audio instruction
briefs regarding forthcoming assignments. Students can then download the audio
file to their device and play it back in their own time. See the *Setting up file downloads*
section in *Chapter 3, Delivering Static Content to Mobiles*, for instructions on how to
upload a file to your course page for access by your students.

Audio files can also be put into an RSS feed, in which case they will be auto-downloaded to students' mobiles as a podcast. See the *Setting up a podcast* section earlier in this chapter for instructions on how to upload an audio file as part of an RSS feed.

Making the audio recording will vary from one device type to another due to the different applications they are shipped with. There are many voice recording apps available in the device app stores including free ones, such as Smart Voice Recorder and Easy Voice Recorder for Android mobile devices. Usage of the actual recording tools is outside the scope of this book, but look for one that allows you to vary the output file type and quality, which will help you to keep the file size as low as possible and optimize it for mobile delivery.

The priority for an audio instruction is accessibility rather than high quality, so you can choose lower sample rates and bit depths than are normally needed, if your recording app allows you alter these values. You also need files that can be read by the majority of audio players on the market, and in particular by mobile devices. You should therefore use a standard, compressed file format that is suited to web delivery, such as MP3.

Providing an audio feedback file

Teachers can use the voice recorder on their mobile device to record audio feedback, which can be more immediate and personal than written feedback. A JISC report titled *Effective Assessment in a Digital Age*, reported that feedback is richer; tutors can expand on salient points, vary the tone, pitch and pace of the voice, and add humor to build rapport, opening the door to an ongoing dialogue between student and tutor. Tutors have found the process convenient and efficient, and even pleasurable. Once a lengthy, time-consuming process, giving detailed feedback now takes place with less effort and in a shorter time.

Audio feedback can then be attached to the assignment feedback so that students can download the audio file to their device and play back in their own time. To enable audio feedback, you will need to adjust the assignment settings to allow feedback files to be uploaded. To do this, perform the following steps:

1. Enter your assignment and then click on **ADMINISTRATION | Assignment administration | Edit settings**.
2. Under **Feedback types**, select the **Feedback files** checkbox.
3. Click on **Save and return to course** or **Save and display**.

The following tasks use screenshots taken from a 7-inch Android tablet:

1. In your course page, click on the assignment activity you wish to grade and click on the **View/grade all submissions** link in the top-right corner.

Audio assignment

Record your audio file on your mobile device and upload your file here.

Grading summary

Participants	2
Submitted	1
Needs grading	1
Due date	Sunday, 22 September 2013, 9:05 PM
Time remaining	14 days

View/grade all submissions

Submission status

Submission status	No attempt
Grading status	Not graded
Due date	Sunday, 22 September 2013, 9:05 PM
Time remaining	14 days

2. On the submitted assignments screen you can click on the link in the **file submission** column to view it and on the **Grade** icon in order to provide your feedback. This table has quite a lot of columns, so even on a desktop computer you need to scroll right to view all the columns. On a mobile device you should simply be able to swipe left and right to view all the columns. In the following screenshot we have turned the mobile device to landscape view to see a wider area and can see the **Submission** and **Grade** columns:

3. Clicking on the **Grade** icon takes you to the submission feedback screen. Here, you can view the submission status, select a grade, provide written feedback, and attach a feedback file. To select a response file, scroll down to the **Feedback files** field and click on the **Add...** button.

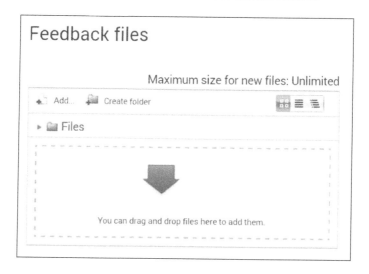

4. The **File picker** window opens. Click on **Choose File**.

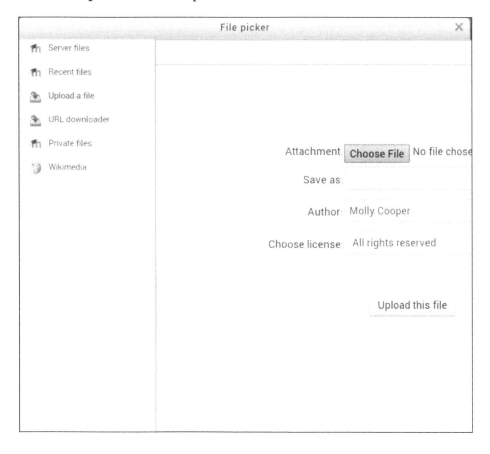

5. At this point, your device's built-in file picker takes over, and you need to pick an action and browse to your feedback file.

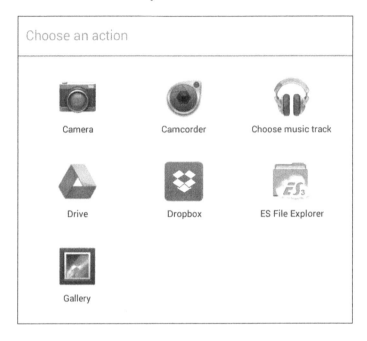

6. Once the file has been selected, it will be listed in the **File picker** screen. You can then click on the **Upload this file** button.

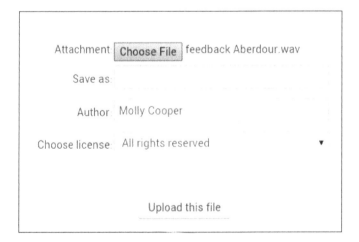

7. The new audio file now appears in the blue box. Click on the **Save changes** button.

Delivering Lecturecasts to mobiles

There are a range of Lecturecast products on the market. These typically consist of hardware and software solutions that record the audio and video components of a lecture. The main consideration of these products for the purposes of mobile learning is in the playback of the lecture recordings through Moodle.

Popular Lecturecast products include:

- Capture Station from Accordent Solutions
- Matterhorn, an open source application from Opencast
- Echo360 from EchoSystems
- CourseCast from Panopto
- Mediasite

At the time of writing, there are various advantages and disadvantages to using some of these products for Moodle-based institutions. For example, Matterhorn has Apple and Android playback apps which is good, and Lecturecasts can be accessed from Moodle, however, a lack of authentication means that links are available to all students and not just those enrolled in the course. Echo360 is Flash-based, while Coursecast and Mediasite are both based on Silverlight, which limits their usage on mobile devices. You will need to research thoroughly which is the right tool for your own institution.

The Lecturecast products listed above have various mechanisms for playing back lecture recordings through Moodle. For example, Panopto has a Moodle block which displays an RSS feed that students can subscribe to, and displays a list of recordings for playback. Panopto content can be displayed within Moodle by using the **Learning Tools Interoperability (LTI)** standard, which both Moodle and Panopto support.

Such blocks will display fine in mobile devices, but you will need to think about block placement, bearing in mind that left blocks appear above the content and right blocks below the content in a single column view. Also remember the rules of mobile device viewing; as a rule of thumb you can expect a learner to engage with a tablet-based task for half an hour, and a smartphone-based task for just a quarter of an hour. With that in mind, lecture playback on smartphones would not be a natural priority, but on tablets it should be.

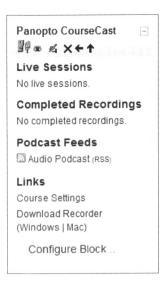

Other considerations to take into account include:

- Be sure to test the quality of the streaming from different connections, such as over 3G, and over institution wireless networks, to test the quality of video streaming

- Check whether lecture playback requires any software plugins, as some—such as Adobe Flash and Microsoft Silverlight—are not mobile friendly

- Does the lecture playback display appropriately on mobile browsers, or alternatively is there an app for playback on mobile devices

Flipping the classroom

It has become increasingly popular in recent years to adopt a "flipped classroom" approach, whereby instead of delivering a lecture to students then asking them to go away and submit a piece of homework, the students view the lecture as the homework before the classroom event, and use the classroom time for discussion and analysis of the lecture. Search online for "flipped classroom" for a wealth of resources and research on this interesting subject.

Creating a video lesson

| **Role**: Tutor | **Time**: 30 minutes and above | **Device**: Desktop |

Many distance learning courses make use of recorded lectures played back as a single recording; however, it is much better practice to split up online lectures into smaller chunks in order to allow time for student reflection. Fortunately, Moodle has an excellent tool for doing just this, called the Lesson activity. A Lesson is a collection of pages incorporating text and media, question screens, and even branching pages that can build up a personal learning path through the activity. Using the Lesson activity for lecture playback allows us to intersperse recorded lecture components with text summary screens and question screens, in order to test understanding before moving on to the next lecture clip.

Remember that while you can upload video files if you wish, Moodle is *not* a streaming media server and it is highly likely that the playback of your video will be slow or stuttering if your site gets busy. For this example, we are embedding video from the MediaCore streaming service and have been provided with a code snippet to embed in the Moodle page.

To create a Lesson activity, perform the following steps:

1. Click on **Add an activity or resource**, and then select **Lesson**.

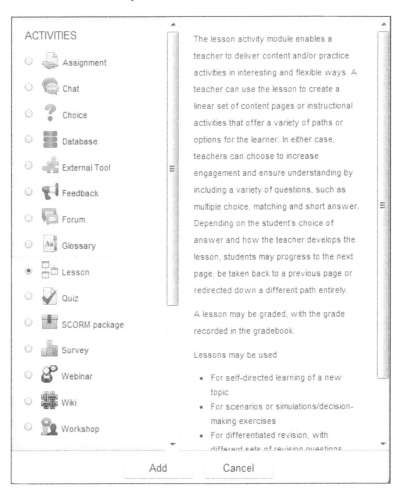

2. In the **Add a new Lesson** screen, there are a number of important fields to complete in order to set the activity up for a lecture recording with interspersed text and question screens. These are as follows:

    °   Under **General**, the **Name** field should contain short and concise name for displaying on a mobile screen

    °   Under **Grade**, the **Grade** field should be set to **No Grade**, and all **Grade** options set to **No**, as we are not scoring this activity

- ○ Under **Flow control**, the **Allow student review** field should should be set to **Yes** so that students can navigate the lesson from the start multiple times

- ○ Under **Appearance**, the **Progress bar** field should be set to **Yes** which shows the completion through the activity beneath the content

3. Click on **Save and display** once all fields are filled in.

4. You will then progress to an empty Lesson activity and need to start populating it with your data. The empty lesson will prompt you to **Import questions**, **Add a content page**, **Add a cluster**, or **Add a question page**.

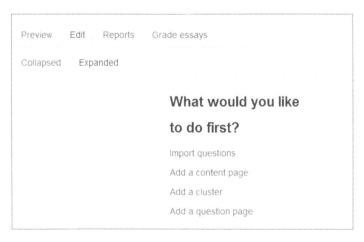

5. We will start by clicking on **Add a content page**.

6. On the **Add a content page** screen, fill in the following fields:

- ○ **Page title**: This should be the title of your page.

- ○ **Page contents**: This provides a HTML editor for you to add your page content. Here we have added an introduction page for the lecture.

- ○ **Arrange content buttons horizontally?**: If selected, it displays the navigation buttons horizontally.

- ○ **Display in left menu?**: If selected, it displays the page on the content menu on the left.

There are then four content field groups, each containing:

- ○ **Description**: This is the text that will appear on the button.

- ○ **Jump**: This is used when we select next page, as we are building a linear path through the pages.

An unlabelled drop-down list in which we select **Moodle auto-format**.

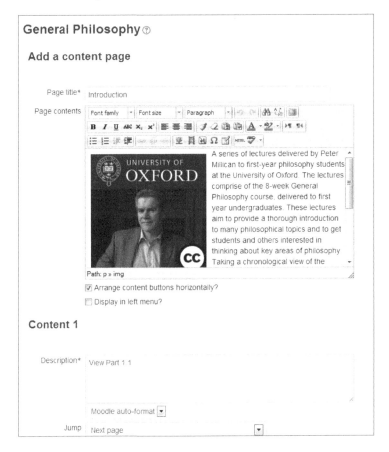

7. Note that as we are just adding a single path through the lesson, we only populate the **Content 1** field.

8. Click on the **Save page** button at the bottom of the form.

9. The page will then be displayed with a number of options, above and below the content item, which allow you to either **Import questions**, **Add a content page**, **Add a cluster**, or **Add a question page here**.

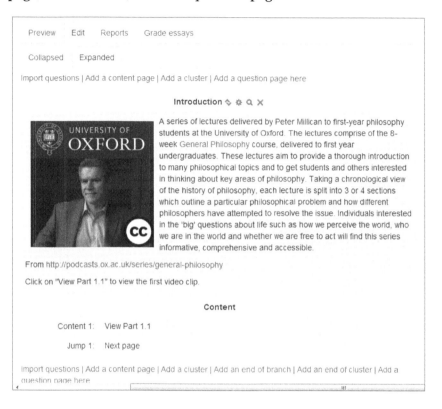

10. We will now go on to add another content page, into which we will add our first lecture clip. In this case we go through the same steps as for the previous screen; however, when we get to the **Page contents** field we need to embed a video clip.

11. Add some introduction text in the HTML editor, and then click on the **Edit HTML Source** button, which is simply labeled **HTML**. This will toggle the view to the **HTML source editor**, where you can add your code snippet. If this is the first time you have ever seen or used the **HTML source editor**, then please do not fear. This tool is normally used by advanced Moodle administrators to add custom code to their pages, but all we are doing in this case is embedding a small code snippet that is provided by the MediaCore streaming service. We do not need to understand what the code means or does, but simply need to embed the snippet into the Moodle page. To do this, we need to go into the HTML source editor as described.

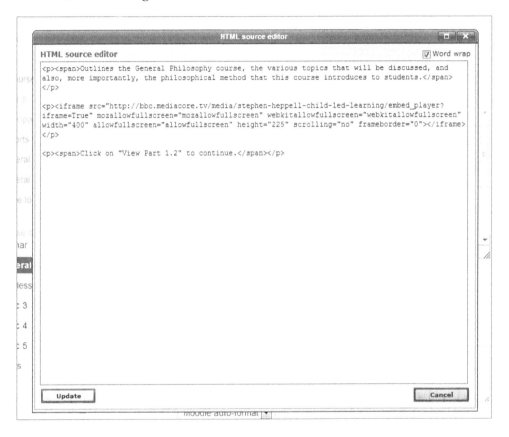

12. Click on the **Update** button, to toggle the view back to **HTML Editor** mode, and you will see your inserted video clip.

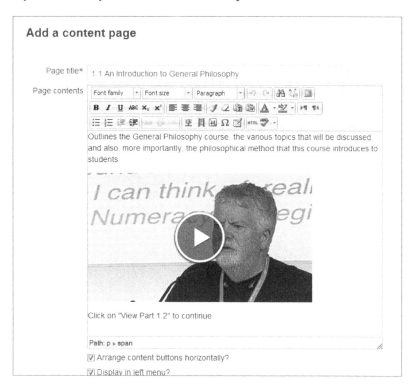

Note that in this example we added some instruction text beneath the video code snippet, which instructs the user to click on the button to continue. It is a good practice to prompt the user like this, but it is your choice as to whether you wish to include such text.

13. Click on **Save page** to continue.

14. We will now add a question screen, before adding our next video clip. First, click on **Add a Question page here**, and then select a **Question Type** from the list.

15. The **Page title** and **Page contents** fields are the same as we have just seen. Enter your question into the **Page contents** field.

16. You can now add up to four answer and response pairs in the fields that follow. Note also that you select the **Multiple-answer** box if you want students to be able to select more than one answer.

17. Below the **Answer** and **Response** fields, you can also select the **Jump** value, which will be the target location of the button following the question. Using the **Jump** button, you can now branch off to different pages depending on the answer selected, or just point all buttons to **Next page** if you have a linear Lesson, such as we are building here.

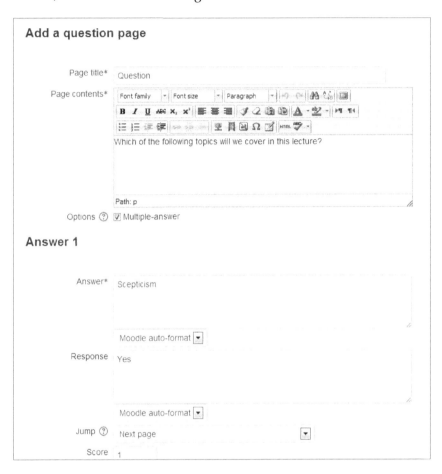

18. Click on **Save page** to continue.

19. Keep adding further pages until you have completed your Lesson activity.

There is a **Preview** tab at the top of the screen, to allow you to see how your Lesson activity will look to your students.

To the student on a mobile device, the Lesson activity will look like the following:

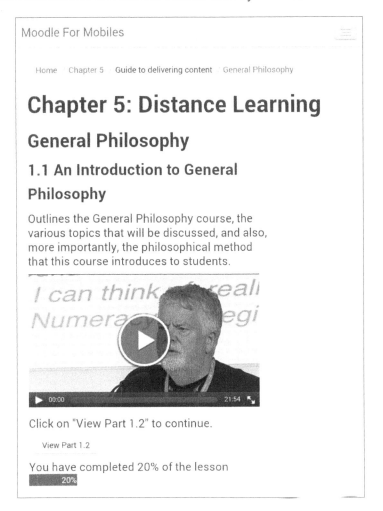

Summary

In this chapter we took a closer look at using multimedia content in Moodle for mobile learning. This focused on audio and video content. Firstly we looked at setting up podcasts in Moodle by using the RSS feature, so that users can subscribe to the Moodle podcast from podcast apps on their mobile devices. We also looked at the use of audio for assignment instruction and feedback.

We then looked at two examples of how video can be used in Moodle for mobile learning. The first was with video lecture casting, where students may wish to catch up on lecture recordings from mobile devices. In the second example, we looked at how video material can be presented to learners by chunking the video up into short clips and adding these into a Lesson activity, with questions between video clips to test knowledge retention. This is an approach that can be preferable to simply uploading a 30 or 60 minute video that runs in full.

In the next chapter we look at assignments in detail, which are another major feature of Moodle that can be tailored for effective mobile delivery.

5
Submitting Audio, Video, and Image Assignments

An important element of mobile learning is using the built-in audio recording and camera capabilities of the mobile devices in students' pockets, enabling them to capture audio, photos, or videos, and upload these into Moodle.

It is important to understand how different file types behave on mobile devices, and certain audio, video, and image file types will require software or apps to view them that may need to be installed on the device.

The possibilities for audio, photo, and video assignments are almost endless. Here are a few ideas to stimulate your thoughts:

Examples of audio assignments include:

- Music assignments
- Oral / language assignments
- Second language assignments
- Interview assignments
- Audio journals
- Presenting a persuasive argument

Examples of video assignments include:

- Taking video of animal movements for biology assignments
- Language assignments
- Role-play assignments
- Sociology assignments

Examples of photo assignments include:

- Photography / art course assignments
- Taking pictures of animals or plants for biology assignments
- Neighborhood landmarks
- Weather and landscape photos for geography assignments

There are a number of options for submission. If all submissions are to be open and public then the database activity is a good idea, and the forum activity is also a possibility. If submissions should remain private, then assignment types requiring the upload of a single file, or advanced uploading of files, would be appropriate. Let's take a look at each of these in turn.

Creating an assignment brief for offline viewing

For all mobile assignments, it makes sense to create an assignment briefing document and upload this as a file into your course page. This will allow your students to download the assignment brief to their mobiles for viewing when they are not logged in, or have no internet connection. See the *Setting up file downloads* section in *Chapter 3*, *Delivering Static Content to Mobiles*, for instructions on how to upload a document to your course page for access by your students.

Setting up an assignment for file submission

1. On your course page, click on **Turn editing on**, and in one of your topic areas, go to **Add an activity or resource** and click on **Assignment**.

2. On the **Adding an Assignment** page, fill in the following fields, as appropriate:

   ° **General | Assignment name**: It is something descriptive, but short and simple.

   ° **General | Description**: This should be recommended that you add some basic instruction text that will be displayed on the course page, rather than using this to add the full assignment brief. For example, "Record your audio file on your mobile device and upload your file here." Keep it short, and then create a separate assignment brief as a document that can be downloaded to students' mobile devices for offline viewing.

   ° **General | Display description on course page**: It is recommended that you select this checkbox so that the brief instruction text is displayed on the course page itself.

   ° **Assignment settings**: This contains a number of fields, such as dates and notifications, which can be set according to your needs, and do not impact mobile usage.

- ° **Submission settings | Online text**: This should be set to **No**, and **File submissions** should be set to **Yes**, as we wish to accept audio file submissions in this case.

- ° **Submission settings | Maximum number of uploaded files** and **Maximum submission size**: These can be set to whatever values you wish. **Maximum number of uploaded files** allows you set limits on how many files your students can upload, which can be useful feature.

- ° **Submission settings | Submission comments**: This can be set to **Yes** or **No**, depending on whether you want students to submit comments alongside their files.

- ° **Feedback settings**: This contains a number of fields regarding how you allow teachers to give feedback; these do not impact on mobile usage.

- ° **Grade | Grade**: This allows you to select any grade from 1 to 100, no grade at all, or scale grade.

- ° **Grade | Grading method**: This contains **Simple direct grading**, along with two more advanced grading mechanisms, **Marking guide** and **Rubric**, which provide more complex assessment forms for criteria-based assessment.

- ° **Grade | Grade category**: This controls the category in which the activity's grades appear in the grade book. By default, this field is empty, and categories need to be added by a teacher.

 For more details on all of these settings, check the following link: `http://docs.moodle.org/24/en/Assignment_settings`

3. Once you have set all required fields, click on **Save and return to course**.

Submitting a file assignment

The tablet view (shown on the right) shows most of the course page, while the smaller smartphone view (shown on the left) just fits the resource and activity on one screen (the user here has scrolled down to this particular entry). Bear in mind, that the amount of scrolling required by the users is dependent on their particular smartphone, so again we have limited the instruction text to the minimum possible.

In order to submit an assignment, the student should perform the following tasks after clicking on the **Assignment** link on the course page

1. Click on the **Add submission** button below the **Submission status** table.

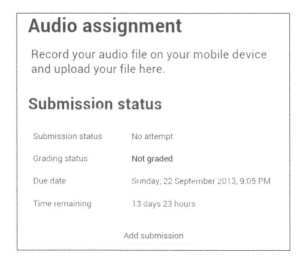

2. There are no files attached yet, so you need to add a file. Do so by either clicking on **Add,** or by dragging a file into the drag-and-drop area, if your browser supports the drag-and-drop of files.

3. The **File picker** window will now open. To upload a file click on the **Upload a file** link on the left and then click on the **Choose File** button.

4. At this point, your device's built-in file picker takes over, and you need to select an action and browse to your file.

5. Once the file has been selected, you can click on the **Upload** this file button and then on the next screen click on the **Save changes** button. The assignment has now been successfully submitted. If this assignment allows multiple submissions then you can click on **Add** again, and select additional files to upload, up to the maximum allowed number (if a limit was set).

6. After clicking on **Save changes**, the **Submission status** page will display the **Submission status** value as **Submitted for grading** and the **File submissions** area will contain a link to the file(s) you have uploaded.

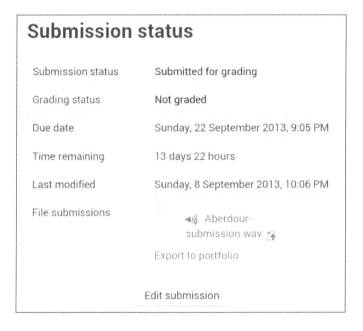

The same task can also performed by using the Moodle Mobile app, by following the following steps:

1. Open the app on your mobile device, and enter your login details on the login screen, as shown in the following (left-most) screenshot:

2. Once logged in to the app, click on **Upload,** and then select either **Photo albums**, **Camera**, or **Audio**, as shown in the following (right-most) screenshot:

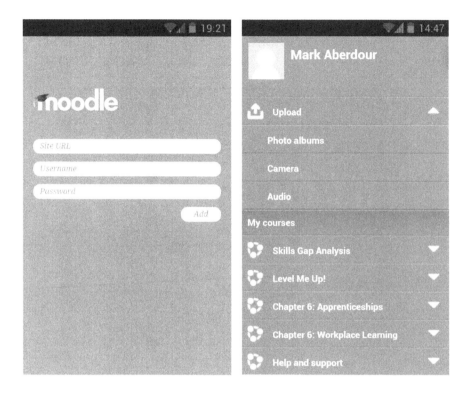

3. Clicking on **Audio** will bring up the built-in voice recorder, and allow you to capture a recording, as shown in the following (left-most) screenshot. There are three buttons at the bottom of the recorder. The left (circle) icon is record, the center (triangle) icon is play, and the right (square) icon is stop. Use the buttons to make your recording, and when you click on stop you will be asked whether to save or discard the recording, as shown in the following (right-most) screenshot:

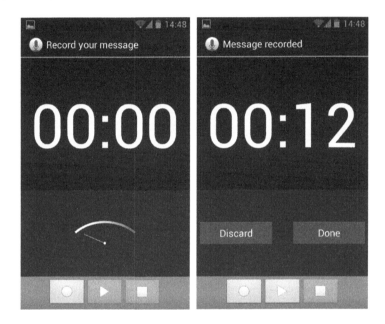

4. When you click on **Done**, the app will upload the recording to the **Private files** area in Moodle and will notify you once the upload is complete, as shown in the following screenshot:

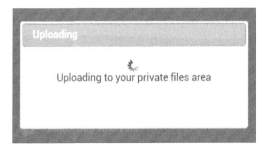

5. The file is now stored in Moodle, but you still need to move it from the **Private files** area in Moodle and submit it as an assignment.

You will need to log in to Moodle directly in order to do this. The Moodle Mobile app does allow you to browse your course and find your assignment, however, at this point it links off to the live site, and will ask you to log in again and then display the live site in the app's built-in browser. It's not a graceful user experience, so you are much better off just opening the site in your standard browser to perform this task. In the future, the mobile app should integrate much more deeply with activities and resources in order to reduce the reliance on a link to the site itself.

To add a file in **Private files** into an Assignment in Moodle, perform the following steps:

1. On the **Assignment** page, click on **Add submission** or **Edit my submission**. In this case we are adding a file to an existing one, so will click on **Edit my submission**.

Submission status

Submission status	Submitted for grading
Grading status	Not graded
Due date	Sunday, 22 September 2013, 9:05 PM
Time remaining	13 days 22 hours
Last modified	Sunday, 8 September 2013, 10:06 PM
File submissions	◀)) Aberdour-submission.wav 📥
	Export to portfolio

Edit submission

2. You will now see the files currently added to the assignment. To add a new one, click on the **Add...** link on the top left of the window, as shown in the following screenshot:

3. This launches the **File picker** pop-up window. On the left of **File picker** there are a number of menu options, including **Recent files**, **Upload a file**, **URL downloader**, **Private files**, and **Wikimedia**. If it is not already selected, click on **Private files**, which is where the Moodle Mobile App has uploaded your recording to.

4. You can then select from the list of files that have been uploaded into the **Private files** area of your Moodle profile.

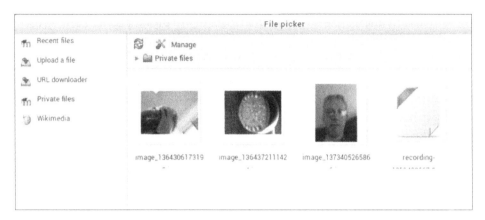

5. When you select one of the files, a new window will display detailed information about the file, and allow you to click on the **Select this file** button to select it.

6. The file will then appear in the main assignment page, alongside the original file, or on its own if was a first upload into a new assignment.

7. Click on **Save changes** to complete the task.

Setting up a Database assignment

The database activity is an excellent choice for submitting the that are to be shared among the class. It allows the students and teachers to build a collection of resources that is fully searchable. It's a very flexible activity with a wide range of configuration options to support almost every conceivable scenario in which you might want to use it.

The large amount of flexibility the database activity affords you does mean that the activity is sometimes perceived as being complicated or difficult to use. It doesn't have to be, though. Perform the following simple steps to set up a database assignment:

1. On your course page, click on **Turn editing on,** and in one of your topic areas, click on **Add an activity or resource**, select **Database,** and then click on the **Add** button.

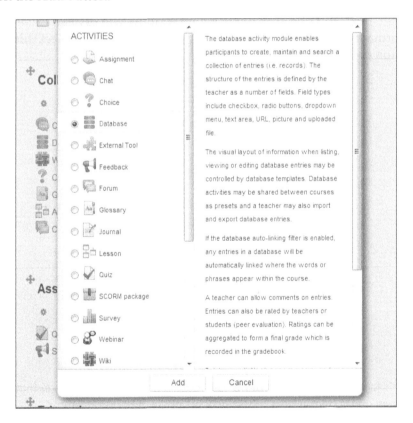

2. On the **Updating database** page, fill in the following fields, as appropriate:

   ° **General | Name**: This should be something descriptive, but short and simple.

   ° **General | Description**: It is recommended that you add some basic instruction text here that will be displayed on the course page, rather than using this to add the actual student brief. For example, "Record your audio file on your mobile device and upload your file here." Create a separate assignment brief as a document that can be downloaded to students' mobile devices for offline viewing.

   ° **General | Display description on course page**: It is recommended that you select this checkbox so that the brief instruction text is displayed on the course page itself.

   ° **General | Available from and to dates**: If your activity requires it, then select dates as needed. You can also make your database read-only by selecting dates for **Read-only from** and **Read-only to**.

   ° **General | Required entries**: This is used if you wish to set the number of entries required of each student.

   ° **General | Entries required before viewing**: This is useful if you want to enforce uploading of a file by students before they can access the other files.

   ° **General | Maximum entries**: This is used if you want to set the maximum number of uploads a student can submit.

   ° **General | Comments**: This is used if you want students to be able to comment on each other's uploads.

   ° **General | Require approval**: If this option is selected, then a teacher must approve each entry before it is displayed.

   ° **Ratings**: This option allows certain users with appropriate permissions to rate each entry.

3. Edit any other fields as you see fit, and then click on **Save and display**.

You now need to set up how the records will be displayed. There are a number of presets and options to choose from; however, for mobile device viewing we suggest the following options are used:

- On the **Fields** tab, you should add the fields that will appear on the upload page. Keep the number of fields low in order to make it easy to upload from a mobile device. In our example, we just have three fields, for **title**, **caption**, and the **audio** file itself. Go to the drop-down box under **Create a new field**, select the field types shown, and fill in the name and click on **Add** for each one. This will create your basic upload form.

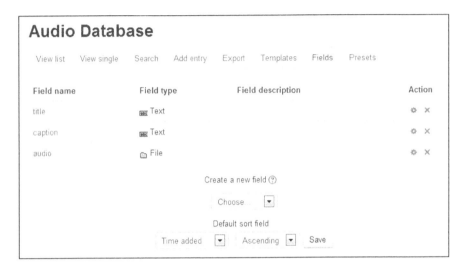

- On the **Templates** tab, you need to at least define the list view, and single entry view. For each view, you can select from a number of placeholder tags that you add to a table in the HTML editor area. This is where it gets a little complicated, but, remember that these are only tables you are setting up, and if you can set up a table in a word document, for example, you can set up a table here. Copy the one given next to try it out, and then make edits from there.

- The **List template** controls how the list of entries will look on the page. Tables with lots of columns do not work well on mobile devices, particularly on the narrow screen of a smartphone, so we suggest using a single column view like the one shown in the following example:

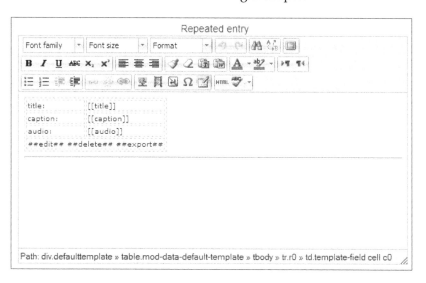

- The **Single template** controls how the entry will look on its own page. Again, we have gone with a single column format, as shown in the following screenshot, which we suggest you copy:

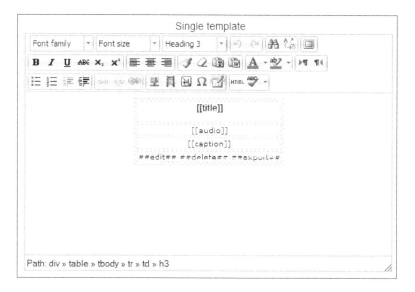

Learner submission of a Database assignment

Perform the following steps to submit a Database assignment:

1. On the course page, click on the **Assignment** link. In this example, we will click on the **Audio Database** activity link.

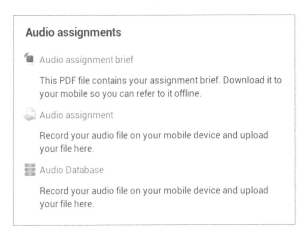

2. We can see that no files have yet been added, as it says **No entries in database**. To add files, click on the **Add entry** link.

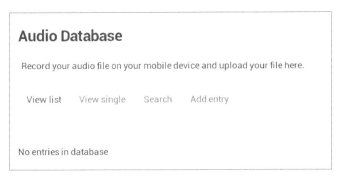

3. You can now enter the **Title** and **Caption** values, and then click on **Add...** to locate your audio file.

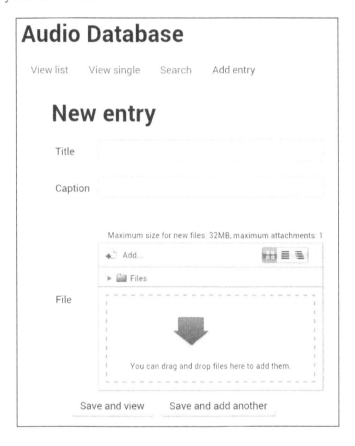

4. The **File picker** window will now open. If the file is already in your Private files area then you can just select it, otherwise click on the **Upload a file** link on the left and click on the **Choose File** button to find your file and upload it.

5. At this point your device's built-in file picker takes over, and you need to select an action and browse to your file.

6. Once the file has been selected, you can click on the **Upload this file** button, after which the new audio file appears in the **File** box. Next, click on the **Save and view** button.

7. The file is now saved, and you are taken to the single entry view of your new entry.

The final result will look something like the following screenshots. The screenshot on the left shows the smartphone view of database activity, while the screenshot on the right shows the tablet view of the same activity:

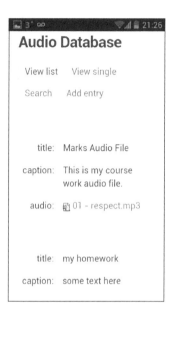

Summary

Mobile devices have built-in functionality for capturing audio, video, and photos, so assignments that allow users to upload files are an excellent way to build mobile learning activities into your teaching. We focused on uploading audio files, but, any of the examples in this chapter could be used for photo or video files too.

In the next chapter we look at another form of knowledge capture: that of reflective logs and journals.

6
Using Mobiles for Capturing Reflective Logs and Journals

In this chapter we will look at the other big use of mobile devices for knowledge capture: **reflective logs** and **journals**. For example, this is a key use of Moodle in apprenticeships and there are a number of activities in Moodle that can be used for keeping reflective logs. These are ideal for mobile learning as reflective log entries tend to be shorter than traditional assignments and lend themselves well to production on a tablet or even a smartphone, especially as the apprentice is very likely to be in a mobile environment in their workplace. Consumption of reflective logs is also perfect for both smartphone and tablet devices as these shorter posts tend to be readable in less than 5 minutes.

Many institutions use Moodle coupled with an **ePortfolio** tool, such as Mahara or Onefile, to manage apprenticeship programs. There are also additional books on ePortfolio tools like Mahara by Packt Publishing should you wish to investigate a third-party, open source ePortfolio solution.

Setting up a reflective log using assignment

Role: Tutor	**Time**: 15 minutes and above	**Device**: Smartphone or Tablet

Using **Assignment** as a reflective log is probably the best tool at our disposal within standard Moodle features. It allows apprentices to repeatedly add reflective notes over time, upload file attachments, and submit the reflective log for assessment. Its only drawback is that the log is a single HTML text area, so the apprentice must remember to date each entry themselves.

To set up a reflective log, perform the following steps:

1. On your course page, click on **Turn editing on** and then, in one of your topic areas, select **Add an activity or resource** and click on **Assignment**.

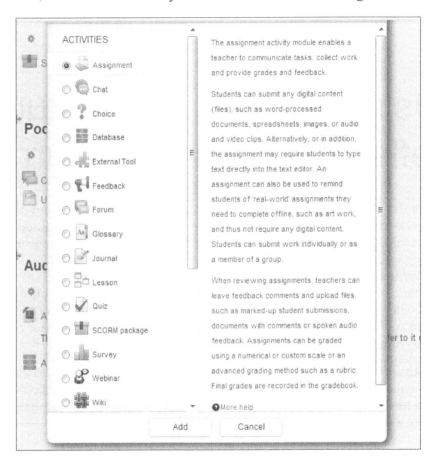

2. On the **Adding a new Assignment** page, fill in the fields as follows:
   - **Submission settings | Require students click submit button**: This can be set to **Yes** so that students can keep an ongoing draft in the system and click on **Submit** only when they are happy that the reflective log is complete and ready for marking.

- ° **Submission types | Online text (Ticked)**: This enables an online text area as well as the uploading of files, allowing the student to enter notes, which is essential for this particular scenario of work placement note taking.

- ° **Submission types | File submissions**: This allows students to upload files.

- ° **Submission types | Submission comments**: Setting this to **Yes** allows students to add comments to their own submissions, which is quite useful for reflective log purposes.

- ° **Submission types | Maximum number of uploaded files**: Up to 20 files can be allowed; it would be useful to select a maximum value here. This could be photos or documents, for example.

- ° **Submission types | Maximum submission size**: Select a high enough setting that reflects the types of uploads you students may be making. For example, if they are uploading video or audio files, select the largest setting.

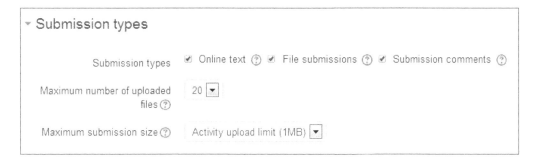

- ° **Grade | No grade**: If you are not submitting your work, it does not require grading.

3. Click on **Save and return to course**.

Submitting a reflective log using assignment

Role: Student	**Time**: 15 minutes and above	**Device**: Smartphone or Tablet

To submit a reflective log, perform the following steps:

1. On the course page click on the assignment link. In this example we will click on the **Reflective assignment** activity link.

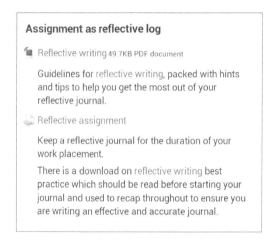

2. We can see that no files have been uploaded and no notes have been added yet. Click on **Add submission**.

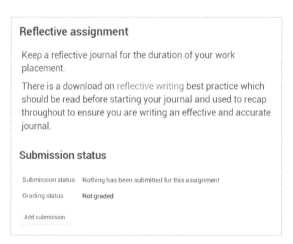

3. The HTML editor now appears and you can start adding some notes, and upload a file if you wish. Once you are done, click on **Save changes**.

4. The notes will then appear on the main page. Your **Submission status** will show as **Draft (not submitted)** and **Grading status** will show as **Not graded**. You can at this point choose to either **Edit my submission** or **Submit assignment**. You can now add further notes and files in a similar manner throughout your placement.

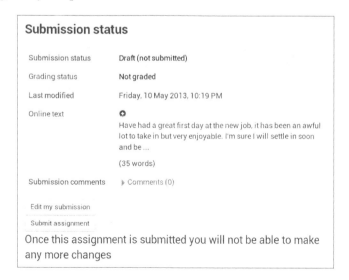

5. Once you are satisfied that the reflective journal is complete, click on **Submit assignment**.

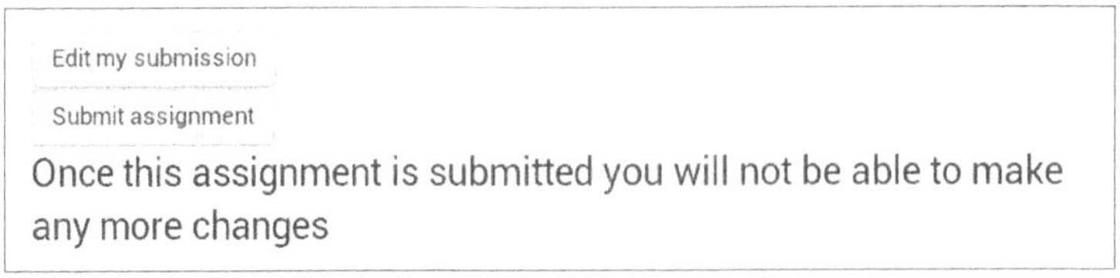

> Edit my submission
>
> Submit assignment
>
> Once this assignment is submitted you will not be able to make any more changes

6. You will then see a confirmation message, at which point you should click on **Continue** to submit your assignment.

7. Your **Submission status** will show as **Submitted for grading**, and the **Grading status** will be **Not graded**.

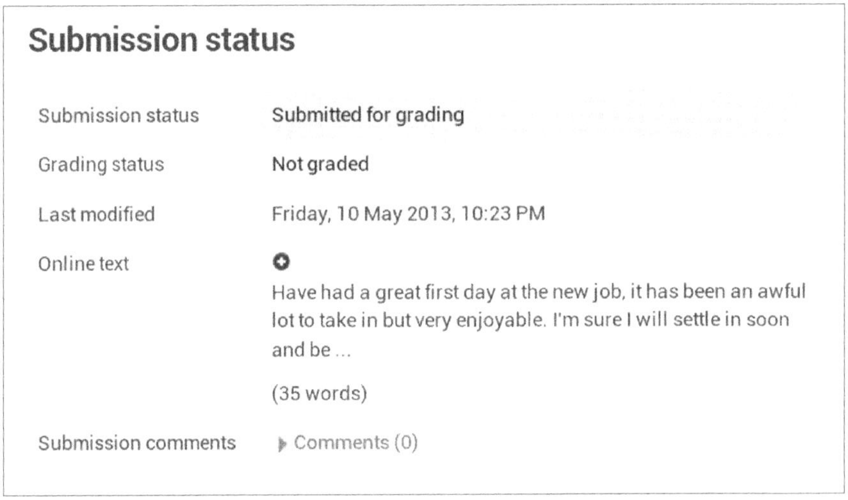

Submission status

Submission status	Submitted for grading
Grading status	Not graded
Last modified	Friday, 10 May 2013, 10:23 PM
Online text	⊙
	Have had a great first day at the new job, it has been an awful lot to take in but very enjoyable. I'm sure I will settle in soon and be ...
	(35 words)
Submission comments	▶ Comments (0)

Grading a reflective log using assignment

Role: Assessor	**Time**: 15 minutes and above	**Device**: Desktop or Tablet

To review and grade a reflective log, perform the following steps:

1. On the course page, click on the assignment link. In this example we will click on the **Reflective assignment** activity link.

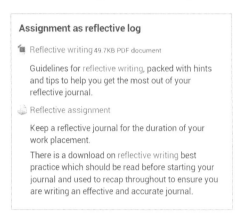

2. On the assignment page you will see the **Grading summary** block. Click on **View/grade all submissions**.

3. You will then see the grading screen, and can view all submitted assignments, edit grades, and add feedback.

4. Click on the **Grade** icon next to the **Submitted for grading** entry. On the **Submission status** screen you can view the assignment submission in full, give it a grade, and add your feedback. Then click on **Save changes**.

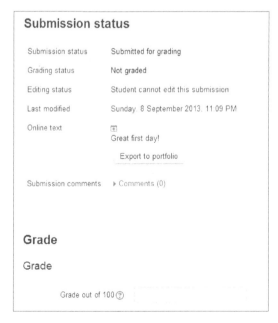

Setting up a reflective log using individual forums

Role: Tutor	**Time**: 5 minutes	**Device**: Desktop

Forums are an excellent way of providing a more informal reflective log, and they are arguably a more usable alternative to the **Assignment** activity because each entry has its own timestamp, and it has support for file attachments. However, individual forums cannot be formally submitted by the apprentice and cannot be closed once complete. They instead provide a journal that is "always open".

To set up a reflective log using individual forums, perform the following steps:

1. On your course page, click on **Course administration | Users | Groups**, and then click on the **Auto-create groups** button.

2. On the **Auto-create groups** page, set **Specify** to **Members of Group** and then set **Group/member count** to **1**. This will set up a group for every individual apprentice, and we can then set up the **Forum** activity for **Separate groups** so that each apprentice sees their own personal forum posts and not anyone else's.

3. On your course page, click on **Turn editing on**, and in one of your topic areas, select **Add an activity or resource**, and then click on **Forum**.

4. On the **Adding Forum** page, fill in the fields as follows:
   ° **General | Forum type** should be **Standard forum displayed in a blog-like format**
   ° **Common module settings | Group mode** should be **Separate groups**
5. Then click on **Save and display**.

Submitting a reflective log using individual forums

Role: Student	**Time**: 15 minutes and above	**Device**: Smartphone or Tablet

To submit a reflective log, perform the following steps:

1. On the course page, click on the assignment link. In this example we will click on the **Reflective log** activity link.

Forum as reflective log

 Reflective forum

Keep a reflective journal for the duration of your work placement.

There is a download on reflective writing which should be read before starting your journal.

2. On first entry, the forum will be empty, so click on the **Add a new topic** button to start your journal.

3. Add text and media using the HTML editor, add file attachments if you wish, and then click on **Post to forum**.

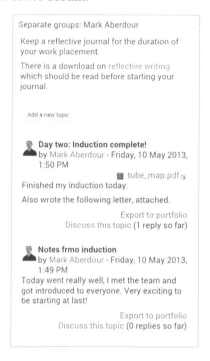

Reviewing a reflective log using individual forums

| **Role**: Assessor | **Time**: 15 minutes and above | **Device**: Desktop or Tablet |

To review and grade a reflective log, perform the following steps:

1. On your course page, click on the **Forum** activity.

2. By default you will see all forum entries, but if you select the **Separate Groups** drop-down menu at the top of the page, you will be able to see all of the groups in the course. Remember that each group is an individual apprentice.

3. At this point you may wish to navigate to **Course administration | Users | Groups** and change the names of the groups to the apprentices' names, as the auto-create group feature gives the groups either letters or numbers as names, not the apprentice name.

4. Select the group and you will then be able to view only the posts for that apprentice.

5. Click on **Discuss this topic** to add a comment to any specific post.

Setting up Moodle for course blogs

Role: Tutor	**Time**: 15 minutes and above	**Device**: Desktop

Course blogs are another way of providing a more informal reflective log. Like the individual forum, each entry has its own timestamp and file attachments are supported, which gives them an edge over assignments in terms of usability. However, as with individual forums, course blogs cannot be formally submitted by the apprentice and cannot be closed once complete. They instead provide a journal that is "always open". Due to the open nature of blogs, they may contravene local laws in some countries for users under a certain age, so check with your legal counsel or manager if in doubt.

Blogs are enabled by default in Moodle. You can change the system-wide blog settings as follows:

1. Click on **ADMINISTRATION | Site administration | Appearance | Blog**.

2. In the **Blog visibility** field there are three options:

   ° **The world can read entries set to be world-accessible**: This is useful if you want to share blog posts with users outside of your site.

- ° **All site users can see all blog entries**: This is the normal setting. Note that you can amend blog accessibility settings by amending the permissions for certain user roles in the **Site administration** settings.

- ° **Users can only see their own blog**: This will help you if you wish the blog posts to remain private.

More advanced settings include the following fields:

- ° **Enable blog associations**: This enables the association of blog entries with courses and course modules.

- ° **Enable external blogs**: This allows a student to import from their external blog's RSS feed if they wish.

- ° **Enable comments**: This allows users to comment on blog posts.

- ° **Show comments count**: This displays the number of comments next to each blog post.

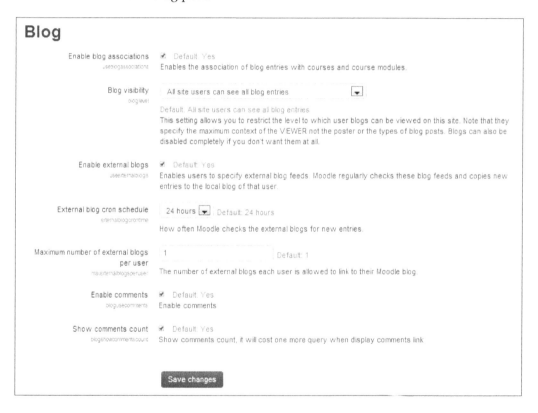

3. Click on the **Save changes** button.

4. Students will now be able to see the **Blogs** menu under **NAVIGATION | My profile**, as follows:

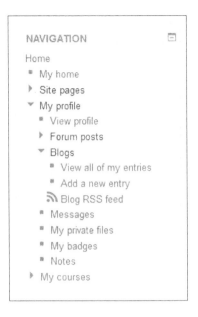

5. Once blogs have been enabled in Moodle, you should add the **Blog Menu** block to your course page by clicking on **Turn editing on** and then selecting **Blog Menu** under the **Add a block** drop-down menu.

Submitting a course blog post

Role: Student	**Time**: 15 minutes and above	**Device**: Smartphone or Tablet

To add a new blog entry, perform the following steps:

1. Click on **NAVIGATION | My profile | Blogs | Add a new entry**.

2. Fill in the blog post with at least a title and body, which are the only two required fields.

3. Add an attachment if you wish.

4. Use the **Publish to** drop-down field to select whether to keep the post as a draft or publish it to anyone on the site.

5. Add tags if you wish. These are useful for collecting together posts from across the course, or even across disciplines on a single topic, for example a particular academic figure, so are well worth using.

6. Click on **Save changes**.

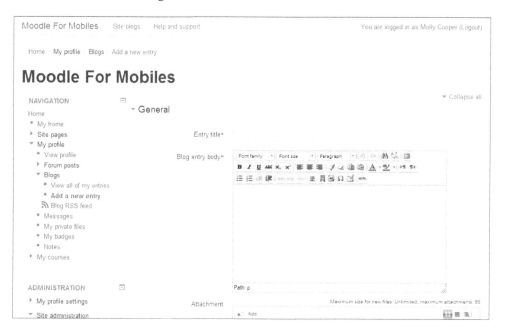

Adding a Blogs link to the site header

Role: Site Administrator	**Time**: 15 minutes and above	**Device**: Desktop

This handy tip will give mobile users quick access to site blogs without having to scroll through the navigation block.

1. Click on **ADMINISTRATION | Site administration | Appearance | Theme settings**.

2. Scroll down to the field **Custom menu items**. You can add menu items into the empty text box. Each line consists of some menu text, a link URL, and a tooltip title, separated by pipe characters.

3. So to add a **Blogs** link you can add the text `Blogs|http://www.moodleformobiles.com/blog/index.php?courseid=0|Site blogs`, replacing `www.moodleformobiles.com` with your own site's homepage URL.

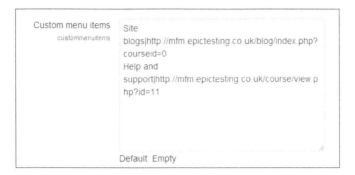

This will display a header bar throughout the site, like the following, which is shown using the Bootstrap theme.

The same view on a mobile device uses the device's menu icon, which is a small square icon in the top-right corner of the device screen. This icon, when clicked on, expands to show a collapsible menu, as shown in the following screenshots. This makes great use of screen space on a mobile device and is a useful way to navigate to key sections of the site.

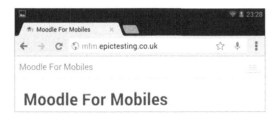

Enabling portfolio export

Role: Tutor	**Time**: 15 minutes and above	**Device**: Desktop

Students in Moodle are able to export their work to an external portfolio system if they wish. To set up your Moodle for portfolio export there are some administrative tasks that you will need to perform, as they are disabled by default in Moodle:

1. Click on **ADMINISTRATION | Site administration | Advanced features**.
2. Select the **Enable Portfolios** checkbox, and then click on **Save changes**.

This will enable support for Portfolios on your Moodle site. You now need to configure the portfolio output settings as follows:

1. Click on **ADMINISTRATION | Site administration | Plugins | Portfolios | Manage portfolios**.
2. On the **Manage portfolios** page, you have a number of options that you can enable and make visible, enable and hide, or disable completely. Note that **Mahara ePortfolio** is disabled by default until **Networking** is enabled in **ADMINISTRATION | Site administration | Advanced features**.

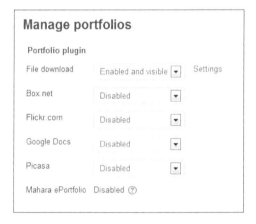

3. When you select each portfolio plugin it will automatically launch a settings page, which you need to fill in and then click on **Save changes**.
4. You can now set the **Common portfolio** settings by navigating to **ADMINISTRATION | Site administration | Plugins | Portfolios | Common portfolio settings**.

5. This page allows you to control how the system behaves when large portfolios are being exported. It is worth consulting with your IT team on the settings to use for this page, as they may differ depending on your network speed and bandwidth.

Exporting your work to a portfolio

Role: Student	**Time**: 5 minutes and above	**Device**: Desktop, Tablet, or Smartphone

When portfolios are enabled, forum posts and other exportable data have an **Export to portfolio** link or icon beside them. Items that may be exported to a portfolio include:

- Assignment submissions — single and multiple file uploads
- Chat sessions
- Database activity entries
- Entire database activities
- Forum posts
- Glossary entries

Any of these individual items can be exported in image, text, HTML, or LEAP2A format. These individual files can then be imported into an ePortfolio tool, such as Mahara, as a piece of evidence in their own right.

To export a forum post you will need to do the following tasks:

1. Each activity type that is capable of being exported to a portfolio will have an **Export to portfolio** link, which the student can click on to initiate the export process.

2. Once clicked you can select the export format, for example, **HTML with attachments** in this case, as we are exporting a forum post with a file attachment.

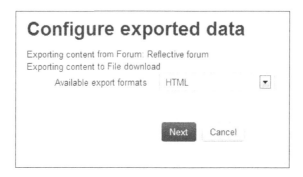

3. The drop-down box may at this point be overridden by the mobile device's own interface for selecting drop-down field values, such as the Android interface shown here:

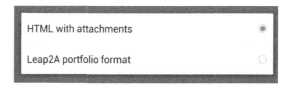

4. Once the format type is selected, you are asked to click on **Continue** in order to confirm that you want to complete the export.

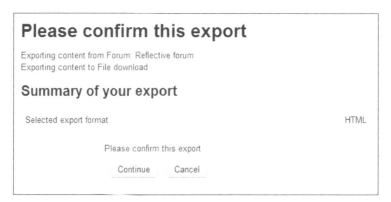

5. There will now be a **Downloading...** message while the item is exported.

6. Check your device download status, for example, on Android you can swipe down from the top edge of the screen to reveal the system notifications that will include a "download complete" message, as shown here.

7. Once downloaded, the file can be imported into an external ePortfolio tool if you wish.

Summary

In this chapter we looked using Moodle for reflective logs and journals. We saw that there are a number of activities in Moodle that can be used for keeping reflective logs and journals, and that these are ideal mobile learning tools for both production by the learner and consumption by their peers or tutors. We looked at assignments, individual forums, and course blogs as reflective log tools, and we also touched on ePortfolio tools and how Moodle work can be exported to an ePortfolio.

In the next chapter we move on to using Moodle for delivering assessments within mobile learning.

7
Performing Assessments Using Mobiles

In this chapter, we look at how a number of different types of assessment tools can built in Moodle by using the quiz activity, and how this can be optimized for mobile learning.

Creating a quiz for formative assessment

There are a range of definitions of formative assessment, but the general approach is one of providing qualitative feedback rather than scores, with the aim of modifying learning activities in order to improve student attainment.

Formative assessment will occur during the learning process rather than at the end of it. In a traditional classroom environment, formative assessment will be used to adjust the teaching to the whole group. However, with online learning we can use the tools within Moodle to adjust teaching for each individual user, for example, by adjusting the individual's learning process and ensuring that each student embarks on a learning path that is uniquely tailored to their individual needs. The techniques we can use in Moodle include:

- End of topic quizzes, to test understanding before moving onto the next topic
- Conditional activities, to lock progress to the next topic until understanding has been demonstrated in the current topic
- Open quizzes, that allow the user to self-assess their understanding, and that include detailed feedback at the question level

Setting up the quiz

Role: Tutor	**Time**: 15 minutes	**Device**: Desktop

To build a formative assessment by using the quiz activity, perform the following steps:

1. Click on the **Turn editing on** button, select **Add an activity or resource**, choose **Quiz** from the drop-down menu, and then click on **Add**.

2. The Quiz settings screen includes the following fields:

    °   **General | Name**: Here we can add a descriptive name for the quiz, but keep it short and simple, such as Unit 1 Self-Assessment.

    °   **General | Description**: Here we can add some basic instruction text for the quiz that will be displayed on the course page, keeping it as short as possible.

- ° **Timing**: This section contains a group of fields that is more useful in summative assessments, so we would usually leave these disabled for a formative assessment.

- ° **Grades**: Similarly, this section also contains a group of fields that is more useful in summative assessments, so we could leave these disabled for a formative assessment. However, you could use the **Highest Grade** (under **Grading method**) setting as an incentive for students to keep trying.

- ° **Layout | Question order**: We would normally set this to **Shuffled randomly** for a formative assessment, so that the student cannot memorize the questions. This relies on using question banks of a large enough size, of course. There may be occasions where you wish to display questions in order, for example, if you are using questions that are built upon one another.

- ° **Layout | New page**: This allows you to select how many questions are displayed per page. Many questions per page is fine for a desktop computer, but on a mobile device where screen space is limited and connectivity is more prone to disruption, it is better to have only one question on each page (using the **Every question** option) in order to minimize page scrolling. This also forces the quiz to save after ever question in case of lost connectivity midway through.

- ° **Question behavior | Shuffle within questions**: This will shuffle options in multiple-choice questions or any other question type with multiple parts, which helps to ensure that the students cannot memorize the right answers. There may be times when you don't want to do this though, for example, if you have answers which include an "All of the above" option in which case this option should always be last.

3. The **Question behavior | How questions behave** field includes a number of options, all of which have distinct uses and are important to get right for formative assessment. The best feedback type for formative assessment, in which we are focused more on feedback than grading, would be **Adaptive mode (no penalties)** which supports multiple tries at each question with hints, or **Immediate feedback** which only allows one chance per question but you can provide feedback after each one. The full list of options are as follows:

   - ° **Adaptive mode**: This allows students to have multiple attempts at a question before moving on to the next one, and provides hints before the student is allowed to try again, with subsequent attempts at a question being awarded fewer marks.

- ° **Adaptive mode (no penalties)**: This is the same as Adaptive mode but does not apply the penalty of fewer marks for multiple question attempts.

- ° **Deferred feedback**: This forces students to answer each question and submit the entire quiz before they receive any feedback.

- ° **Deferred feedback with CBM**: This includes Certainty-Based Marking (CBM), whereby the student indicates how certain they are that they got the question right. This grading then takes the certainty into account; so that students are penalized for guessing an answer which turned out to be correct, or were very confident about their answer, but subsequently got it wrong.

- ° **Immediate feedback**: This forces students to submit each question as they go along to get immediate feedback, but they only get one chance at each question.

- ° **Immediate feedback with CBM**: This again includes the Certainty-Based Marking concept for this particular feedback type.

- ° **Interactive with multiple tries**: This forces students to submit each question as they go along to get immediate feedback, and if they do not get it right then they can have another try for fewer marks.

4. The Quiz settings screen includes a number of field groups under **Review options**. These allow you to set detailed feedback options at the following four stages:

    - ° **During the attempt**: This will only display the feedback if the appropriate feedback types are selected under **How questions behave**.

    - ° **Immediately after the attempt**: This will display the feedback for the first two minutes after **Submit all and finish** is clicked.

    - ° **Later, while the quiz is still open**: This will display the feedback until the quiz close date.

    - ° **After the quiz is closed**: This will display the feedback after the quiz close date has passed. If the quiz does not have a close date, this state is never reached.

5. Each of the four groups mentioned in the above step contain the same set of the following fields which can be ticked or unticked depending on your preference as a teacher:

    ° **Whether correct**: This will display whether the answer to the question was correct, partially correct, or incorrect

    ° **Marks**: This will display the marks awarded for the answer

    ° **Specific feedback**: This will display the feedback for the particular answer that the student entered, for example, a multiple-choice question with four possible answers

    ° **General feedback**: This will display the feedback for the whole question and will be seen by all students irrespective of the marks they got for that question, which is good for fully-worked answers with links to further information

    ° **Right answer**: This will show the correct response, but can be turned off if you wish to provide a full explanation of the correct answer in the general feedback instead

    ° **Overall feedback**: The response will be displayed at the end of the attempt and is tailored for specific grade ranges

6. Together, all of these feedback options provide a tremendous level of flexibility and allow you to tailor your quiz to the circumstances in which it is to be delivered. For a typical formative assessment, we would suggest selecting the following set of options as a starting point for your quiz, and then adjusting as you see fit for your own circumstances:

7. The remaining field groups can be left with the default settings, although one final important group remains: **Overall feedback**. This is where you can set the feedback for the whole attempt, within certain grade boundaries, so that students may receive overall quiz feedback that is appropriate to their level of attainment.

8. Once you have filled in all of the fields, click on **Save** to submit the quiz settings, and then you can start actually building the quiz itself.

Building a question bank

Role: Tutor	**Time**: 30 minutes and above	**Device**: Desktop

With a formative assessment, it is better to create a question bank from which random questions can be drawn into the actual quiz. To create a question bank, perform the following steps:

1. Navigate to **ADMINISTRATION | Quiz administration | Question bank**. Select the question bank category from the drop-down list. You can select a question bank just for this specific quiz, for the wider course, category, or full system. For this self-assessment, we will build a question bank for just this specific quiz. The remaining fields can all be left with their unselected default states, unless you wish otherwise.

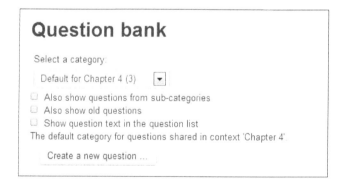

2. Click on the **Create a new question...** button. You can now select the question type from a list of 11 question types that come as standard with Moodle. We will set up a simple question by selecting the **Multiple choice** question type option, and then clicking on **Next**.

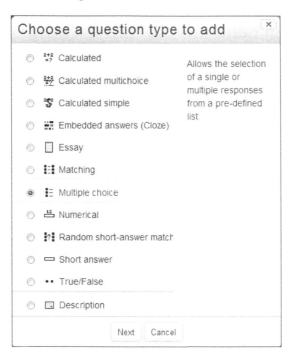

3. We can now populate our question with, among other fields, the following information:

    ° **Question name**, which will be displayed in the question bank, so make it easily identifiable

    ° **Question text**, which will be displayed to the student

    ° **General feedback**, which is mentioned previous section, and should be applied to the whole question and it will be seen by all students irrespective of the marks they got for that question, so use this for full answers with links to further information

    ° For each choice, we can define an answer, grade, and specific feedback

4. Click on **Save Changes** to save the question into the question bank.

5. Continue to add questions to your question bank until you have reached a number from which a quiz can be constructed. There are a lot of question types available in Moodle; however, there are additional question types and behaviors available as Moodle plugins.

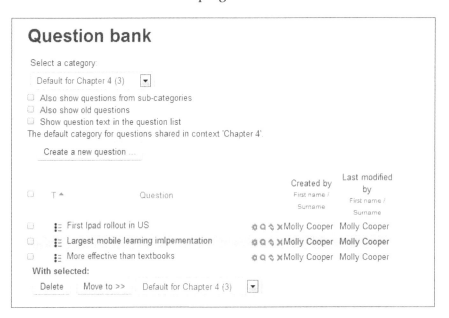

Building your quiz

| **Role**: Tutor | **Time**: 15 minutes | **Device**: Desktop |

The key concepts to remember when building a quiz are: a quiz contains a number of questions split over one or more pages, and those questions can be added to a quiz directly, or pulled in from a question bank either randomly or selectively. There are a number of question types to choose from. Note that once your quiz is in operation, you are not able to change how it is built, so ensure that you have set it up correctly before releasing it to your students.

To build your quiz, perform the following steps:

1. Navigate to **ADMINISTRATION | Quiz administration | Edit quiz**. This will display the **Editing quiz** screen.

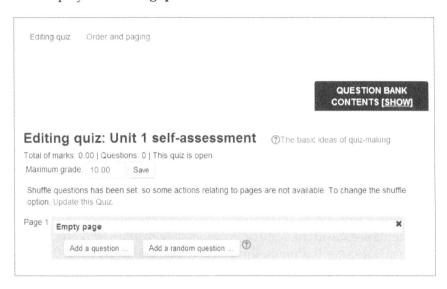

2. To add a random question from the question bank, click on the **Add a random question...** button.

3. This will launch a modal window in which you can select the question bank category and click on the **Add random question** button.

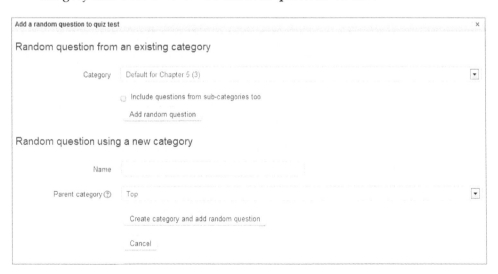

4. The random question will then be added into the quiz. You can now add further random questions or specific questions into the quiz as you see fit.

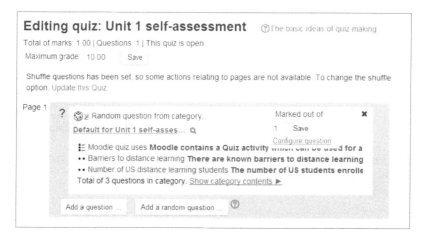

5. Questions are saved int.o the quiz automatically after each one is created, so there is no save button on this screen. Navigate away from the screen, for example, by clicking on your course name in the main navigation, in order to get back to your course page.

Accessing your quiz

Role: Student	**Time**: 15 minutes and above	**Device**: Smartphone or Tablet

From the student perspective, to create a newly-constructed quiz, perform the following steps:

1. Select the quiz activity on the Moodle course page. This will be preceded by the check-mark icon as shown in the following screenshot, and possibly by the quiz description if selected to display on the course page:

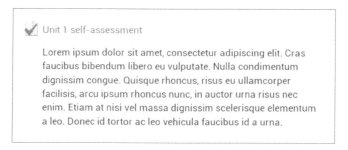

2. Once in the activity, the quiz description is displayed and the student can click on the **Attempt quiz now** button.

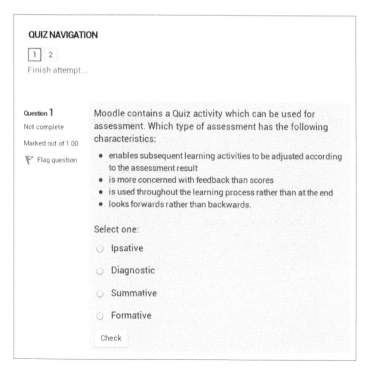

3. Each question appears in the format as shown in the following screenshot, with the quiz questions spanning the top portion of the screen. Below this is the question status data on the left, and the actual question on the right. As we have built our quiz to get immediate feedback after each question, there is a **Check** button after the question.

4. Feedback that relates to the answer selected is then given, and beneath that the general feedback for the entire question is displayed. The displaying of specific and general feedback is due to the fact that we selected these options on the Quiz settings screen.

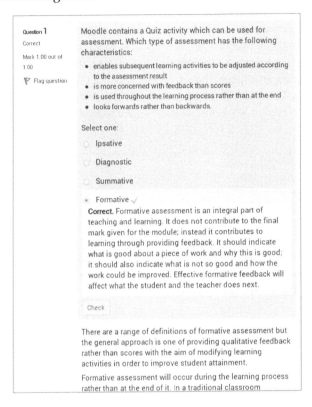

5. Once all questions are completed, click on **Submit all and finish**.

6. There is then a **Confirmation** message, at which point the user should click once again on **Submit all and finish**.

7. Due to the options that we selected in the Quiz settings screen, we now see the overall feedback as well as the individual question feedback again. At the bottom of the screen, we can click on **Finish review**.

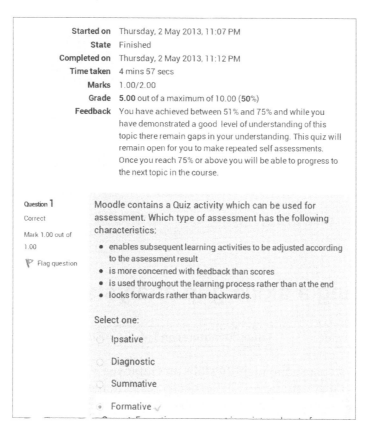

8. We then go to the Quiz introduction page. This displays each attempt over time and its associated grade and feedback, followed by the overall feedback for the highest grade. The following screenshot shows how this quiz is set up:

Summary of your previous attempts

Attempt	State	Marks / 2.00	Grade / 10.00	Review	Feedback
1	Finished Submitted Thursday, 2 May 2013, 11:12 PM	1.00	5.00	Review	You have achieved between 51% and 75% and while you have demonstrated a good level of understanding of this topic there remain gaps in your understanding. This quiz will remain open for you to make repeated self assessments. Once you reach 75% or above you will be able to progress to the next topic in the course.
2	Finished Submitted Thursday, 2 May 2013, 11:31 PM	2.00	10.00	Review	Well done, you have achieved over 75% and have demonstrated a high level of understanding of this topic. While this quiz will remain open for you to make repeated self assessments if you wish, you are now able to progress to the next topic in the course. Congratulations!

Highest grade: 10.00 / 10.00.

Overall feedback

Well done, you have achieved over 75% and have demonstrated a high level of understanding of this topic. While this quiz will remain open for you to make repeated self assessments if you wish, you are now able to progress to the next topic in the course. Congratulations!

Re-attempt quiz

Performing a skills gap analysis

Role: Tutor	**Time**: 30 minutes and above	**Device**: Desktop

Skills gap analysis is used to identify skills an employee should have but may not adequately meet the required level in order to perform their job effectively. A series of questions will be organized into topics, and tasks and the results will indicate where the skills gaps are for an individual, department, or organization. Training plans can then be put into place, ideally by automatically linking to resources relating to the user's skills gaps, in order to build a personal learning path for each user that adapts to the individual's own skills gaps.

Skills Gap Analysis

Quality orientation

This competency is about delivering excellence through high quality and standards that match the requirements of the business.

Choice 1 Pages 2

Progress: 1 / 2

Customer focus

This competency is about putting the customer first (be they internal or external) and being eager to provide legendary service by working to identify, meet and then exceed their needs at every opportunity.

Quiz 1 File 1 URL 1

Progress: 1 / 3

Continuous Improvement

This competency is about taking personal responsibility for recognising and responding to own development needs and actively seeking out opportunities to learn from situations and colleagues.

For organizations with a largely mobile workforce, such as sales staff or field engineers, it is important that these staff can perform their skills gap analysis on mobile devices. To perform skills gap analysis, follow the following steps:

1. Navigate to **ADMINISTRATION | Course administration | Edit settings**.

2. Under **General**, select **Topics format** as the value for **Course format**.

3. Under the formatting options, for **Topics format** select the following:

    ° **Number of sections**: Here we select **3** as we are setting up three skills, but you can choose whatever number you wish here.

    ° **Course layout**: Here we select **Show one section per page**. This allows each level to have its own distinct identity and set of resources, if you wish.

4. Navigate to **Completion tracking | Enable completion tracking**, select **Yes**.

This will set up your course settings correctly. There are no hidden topics on this course, so we will have all competencies available on the course page, and the competency title can be clicked on in order to enter the actual page, which is a course section.

Within each competency section, you now need to set up the competency description, diagnostic tool, and associated resources. To do this, perform the following steps:

1. Click on **Add an activity or resource** and select **Label**.

2. In the HTML editor, add your competency description text. This will likely be a bulleted list of behaviors associated with that competency.

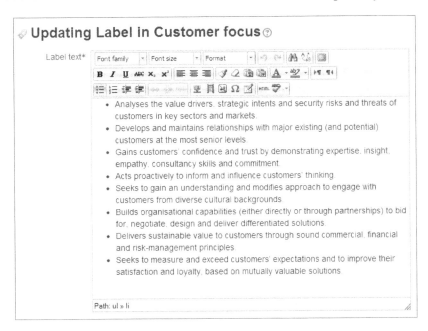

3. There are some additional settings on this page under **Restrict access**; however, you should leave all these alone as we do not wish to restrict access to this label. Under **Activity completion**, you should select **Do not indicate activity completion**, as this label is really just supporting text and we do not need to track a completion status for it.

4. Add a competency diagnostic tool. For this, we will use the quiz activity. We have already seen elsewhere in the book how to set up a quiz activity so there is no need to repeat the steps here. The important parts of the quiz setup, however, are as follows:

    ◦ **Grade | Attempts allowed**: Here we will select **Unlimited** as we want users to be able to come back and perform the diagnostic again, at any point, as their skills and expertise improve over time.

    ◦ **Grade | Grading method**: Here we will select **Last attempt**, which will ensure that the learning resources we release following the diagnostic completion relate to the employee's current results, and not to their previous or average results.

    ◦ **Question behavior | How questions behave**: Here we will select **Deferred feedback**, which will ensure that the feedback is delayed until the end of the diagnostic.

- ° **Review options | During the attempt**: This option will be grayed out due to selecting **Deferred feedback** previously.

- ° **Review options | Immediately after the attempt**: This option should just have **Marks** and **Overall feedback** selected, as the release of particular learning resources is really a form of feedback, rather than having written feedback for specific questions, for example.

- ° The same options should be applied to **Later, while the quiz is still open** and **After the quiz is closed**.

- ° **Overall feedback | Grade boundary**: This should be set to the point at which you want to release different sets of resources. For example you could have boundaries at `25%`, `50%`, and `75%`, in which case you would have four sets of learning resources depending on the employee's score. Give each grade boundary its own feedback text, such as, `You failed the assessment however you scored between 51 and 75% so you are nearly there. Review the suggested materials on the course page and try again.` or `Well done, you have demonstrated that you can perform this behavior to the required standard,` for users who achieve over 75 percent.

- ° **Restrict access**: We do not have any restrict access conditions set for this diagnostic tool.

- ° **Activity completion | Completion tracking**: Select **Show as complete when conditions are met**, and select the **Student must receive a grade to complete this activity** field, which will ensure that the diagnostic is marked as complete once the employee has achieved a grade upon completing it.

5. Click on **Save and return to course**.

The preceding quiz settings will result in your competency section looking like the one shown in following screenshot. The page now takes the format of an initial competency description, with the summary in the section title and the detailed bullets as a separate label. In this way, only the high-level summary is shown on the main course page to avoid it becoming too text-heavy.

Quality orientation   **Customer focus**   Continuous Improvement▶

This competency is about putting the customer first (be they internal or external) and being eager to provide legendary service by working to identify, meet and then exceed their needs at every opportunity.

Your progress ⑦

- Analyses the value drivers, strategic intents and security risks and threats of customers in key sectors and markets.
- Develops and maintains relationships with major existing (and potential) customers at the most senior levels.
- Gains customers' confidence and trust by demonstrating expertise, insight, empathy, consultancy skills and commitment.
- Acts proactively to inform and influence customers' thinking.
- Seeks to gain an understanding and modifies approach to engage with customers from diverse cultural backgrounds.
- Builds organisational capabilities (either directly or through partnerships) to bid for, negotiate, design and deliver differentiated solutions.
- Delivers sustainable value to customers through sound commercial, financial and risk-management principles.
- Seeks to measure and exceed customers' expectations and to improve their satisfaction and loyalty, based on mutually valuable solutions.

 Customer focus diagnostic tool

Complete this diagnostic tool. Depending on the answers you give, a set of appropriate resources will be displayed for you to complete. You can return to this diagnostic at any time and test your yourself again. Ultimately we want our employees to achieve the highest level of competence.

Beneath the competency description, we then have our competency diagnostic tool, which has a number of questions relating to this particular competency. Your organization should decide on the type and number of questions needed in order to determine what level of competence the employee is performing at.

We now need to set up the resources that will be displayed when the employee achieves a certain score in the diagnostic.

To set up the resources, perform the following steps:

1. Under the diagnostic quiz, add a new **Label** resource. Repeat the steps performed earlier in this section to add the actual label. You will want to add some text such as, `Your last attempt at the diagnostic tool resulted in a score of between 51 and 75%. This demonstrates a good understanding of what is required for this competency. Review the suggested materials below and then repeat the diagnostic when you feel ready..`

2. Go to **Restrict access | Grade condition**, select the **Customer focus diagnostic tool** from the drop-down list, then set the following fields: **must be at least** to `51` % and **and less than** to `76` %.

3. Go to **Restrict access | Before activity can be accessed**, select **Hide activity entirely** so that only the appropriate message appears for the employee. Otherwise, the alternate messages will appear grayed out rather than hidden.

4. Under **Completion tracking**, do not indicate activity completion as this is simply an instructional message and does not require a completion status.

5. Add resources and activities aimed at users who scored between 51 and 75% for this competency. In the activity or resource settings, use identical restrict access conditions as for the label you set up in steps 1 to 3. We would most likely opt to turn Activity completion on for the resources and activities, in order to track who has completed which items.

Repeat the preceding process for each grade range. For example, you could add a targeted instruction label and learning resources for 0 to 25%, 26 to 50%, 51 to 75% and 76 to 100% ranges. To make course administration easier, it is worth grouping these together so that you have a label and resources for 0 to 25 %, followed by a label and resources for 26 to 50% and so on.

The end result is a page that displays like the one shown in following screenshot. In this case, the employee has scored between 26 and 50% in the diagnostic tool, so an appropriate instruction message is displayed, followed by the learning resources that relate to that particular grade range.

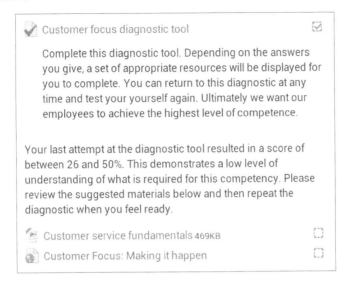

Using this technique, you can build a course based around your organization's core competencies. Each employee can engage in learning resources and activities that are relevant to their level of competence.

Creating a quiz for summative assessment

Summative assessments provide students with a score in order to summarize their educational development at the end of a learning unit. In traditional classroom learning this would be a paper exam, whereas in distance learning it takes the form of an online assessment. While Moodle's quiz activity has a great deal of flexibility and lends itself well to being used as a learning tool, it can also be used for summative assessment if set up appropriately.

However, online summative assessment does come with risks. Users are not in a formal examination environment, so there is more scope for cheating. There are tools in Moodle quiz that we can use to mitigate this risk, including:

- Opening and closing a quiz at a specific time. This goes against the scheduling flexibility that many turn to distance learning to take advantage of, although a quiz could realistically be opened on a weekly or monthly basis for summative assessment.

- Timed quizzes, which reduces the possibility of users going away and finding answers to questions.

- Secure windows, which reduce the possibility of users tabbing to a browser window to look online for answers, although of course users may still have a smartphone or tablet by their side.

- Making the quiz only accessible by entering a secure password that is released at the time the quiz starts.

- Monitoring students in physical, class-based assessments, or using monitoring tools, such as ProctorU for assessments on distance-learning courses, which uses a webcam to monitor students.

Setting up the quiz

Role: Tutor	**Time**: 15 minutes	**Device**: Desktop

To build a summative assessment using the Quiz activity, perform the following steps:

1. Click the **Turn editing on** button, select **Add an activity**, choose **Quiz** from the drop-down menu, and then click on **Add**.

2. The Quiz settings screen can be set up as previously described for a formative assessment, with the following changes:

   - **Grade | Attempts allowed**: This should be set to 1.

   - **Time | Open and close the quiz by date**: This is particularly useful for setting the quiz to only be available on a certain date and time.

   - **Time | Time limit**: It allows a limit, in minutes, to be set for the quiz duration once the user starts the quiz.

   - **Time | When time expires**: This provides options for how to handle the time limit expiry, including not counting unsubmitted attempts, offering a grace period for submission but no more answers, and submitting open attempts automatically.

   - **Question behavior | How question behave**: This should have a different selection for a summative assessment, most likely either **Adaptive** mode to allow multiple attempts at questions with hints but fewer marks for subsequent attempts, **Deferred feedback** to submit the entire quiz before students receive any feedback at all, or **Deferred feedback with CBM** which includes Certainty-Based Marking, whereby the student indicates how certain they are that they got the question right. This grading then takes the certainty into account, so that students are penalized for guessing an answer which turned out to be correct, or were very confident about their answer but subsequently got it wrong.

○ **Review options**: This will look something like the following screenshot for a summative assessment with much more limited feedback provided.

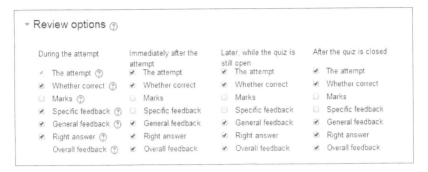

○ Under **Extra restrictions on attempts**, click on the **Show more** link to reveal all the fields

○ **Browser security**: This offers **Full screen pop-up with some JavaScript security**, which basically means that the quiz appears in a full screen pop-up window that covers all of the other windows and has no navigation controls, and students are prevented, as far as is possible, from using features such as copy and paste.

Accessing your quiz

Role: Student	**Time**: 15 minutes and above	**Device**: Smartphone or Tablet

From the student perspective, the newly constructed quiz will look quite different from the previous formative quiz we set up. Perform the following steps to set up the summative assessment:

1. Select the quiz activity on the Moodle course page. This will be preceded by the check-mark icon as shown in the following screenshot, and possibly by the quiz description if selected to display on the course page.

> ✓ Unit 1 final assessment
>
> Lorem ipsum dolor sit amet, consectetur adipiscing elit. Phasellus elit erat, malesuada ornare euismod non, egestas vel elit. Phasellus fringilla viverra nisl non aliquam. Nunc sed neque eu massa tincidunt convallis et sed augue. Etiam vitae justo diam. Proin fringilla accumsan laoreet.

2. Once in the activity, the quiz description is displayed along with the notification of a single attempt and the time limit. The student can click on the **Attempt quiz now** button.

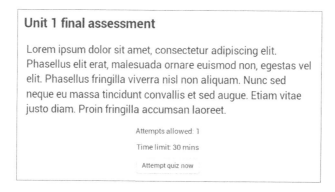

Unit 1 final assessment

Lorem ipsum dolor sit amet, consectetur adipiscing elit. Phasellus elit erat, malesuada ornare euismod non, egestas vel elit. Phasellus fringilla viverra nisl non aliquam. Nunc sed neque eu massa tincidunt convallis et sed augue. Etiam vitae justo diam. Proin fringilla accumsan laoreet.

Attempts allowed: 1

Time limit: 30 mins

Attempt quiz now

3. A **Confirmation** message is displayed, because only a single attempt is allowed.

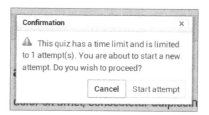

4. Each question appears in the format as shown in the following screenshot, with the quiz questions spanning the screen. Below this is the question status data on the left, and the actual question on the right. As we have built our quiz to get deferred feedback at the end, there is a **Next** button after the question, rather than the **Check** button, as we saw in the previous sections.

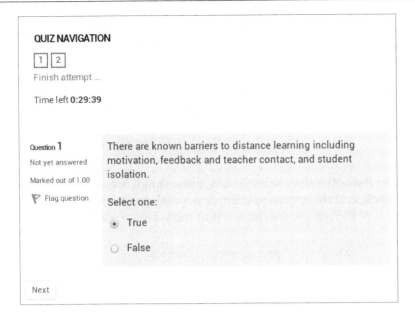

5. Once all questions are submitted, the student will click on **Submit all and finish**.

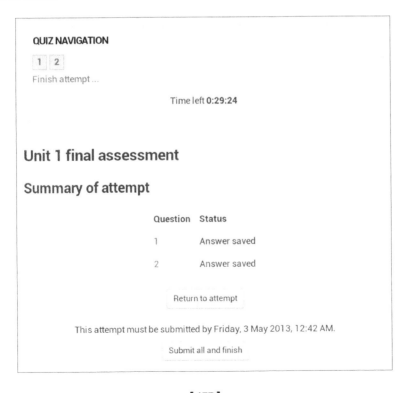

6. There is a final confirmation prior to quiz submission, and the student must click on **Submit all and finish**.

7. Due to the options we selected in Quiz settings, we only see the overall feedback, and do not see specific or general question feedback. At the bottom of the screen, we can see that there are no more attempts allowed:

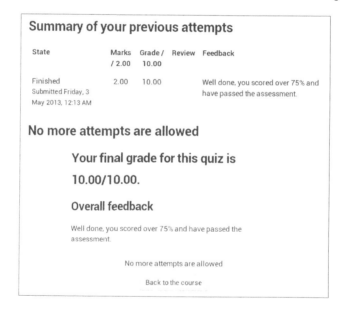

Checking grades

Quick tasks, such as checking grades, are a prime candidate for mobile access.

Navigate to **Site administration** | **Grades** | **Report settings** to select the columns to display for each report, in order to optimize the report for mobile delivery. You should aim to reduce the columns shown to the minimum required by your students. For example, under **User report**, you can select from the following columns:

- **Show rank**
- **Show percentage**

- **Show grades**
- **Show feedback**
- **Show ranges**
- **Show weightings**
- **Show average**
- **Show letter grades**

The default columns on tablet and smartphone are shown in the following screenshots. Obviously, on the smaller devices, a relatively high number of columns will negatively impact the display.

Summary

In this chapter, we looked at how a number of different types of assessment tools can built in Moodle using the quiz activity and how these can be optimized for mobile learning. We looked specifically at formative and summative assessments, and demonstrated how to build a skills gap analysis with personalized learning paths which is a common requirement for workplace learning.

In the next and final chapter, we shall look at how to use Moodle's communication tools within a mobile learning context.

8
Communicating with Mobile Users

In this chapter we look at communication—one of Quinn's 4 Cs of mobile learning. Moodle has a wide range of communication tools and we explore how these can be used in a mobile learning context.

Setting up a group discussion

Online communication tools are split between synchronous (where users interact in real-time, such as in a chat room) and asynchronous (where users interact over multiple browser sessions, such as a discussion forum). Asynchronous tools are really useful for mobile learning when users can reasonably be expected to be online at different times but may wish to access and contribute to the discussion at any time of day—especially if it's homework or assessment related. Moodle discussion forums can also be subscribed to by e-mail, so that daily updates can be pushed out to subscribers, which is really useful for mobile learners.

Whether you choose to set up a forum for course related activity or not, it is a good idea to create a mobile technical forum on which students can share their expertise and interest, and help to solve each other's problems.

To set up a group discussion forum, perform the following steps:

1. On your course page, click on **Turn editing on**, then in one of your topic areas select **Add an activity or resource**, and then click on **Forum**.

2. On the **Adding a new Forum** page, there are a range of fields to fill in that includes the following:

    Under the **General** subheading, specify the following:

    ○ **Forum name**: This is kept short for viewing on mobile devices

    ○ **Description**: This is also kept short, if you are selecting **Display description on course page,** otherwise you can make it as long as you like

    ○ **Forum type**: Here there are a number of options, of which we will choose **Standard forum for general use**

Under the **Subscription and tracking** subheading, do the following:

- Subscription mode: This allows users to receive e-mail copies of forum posts. It is usually best to let the user decide, so we would recommend selecting **Optional subscription** from the drop-down list. There are alternatives such as **Forced subscription** where everyone is subscribed and has no option to unsubscribe, **Auto subscription** in which is everyone is subscribed but can unsubscribe if they wish, and **Subscription disabled** in which case the user has no option to subscribe at all.

Under the **RSS** subheading, do the following:

- RSS feed for this activity: This is a good option to select as some mobile users will use RSS readers to keep up-to-date with news sites; so this allows them to include course discussions in their personal tools

3. Click on **Save and display**.
4. You will now be in an empty forum, so the first thing you should do is write an introductory post. Click on the **Add a new discussion topic** button.

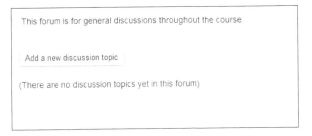

5. You can now fill in your discussion topic. The first two fields are red with an asterisk which means they are required fields. Click on **Post to forum** when you have finished writing your entry.

6. You will now be returned to the forum page, and your first post will be ready to view:

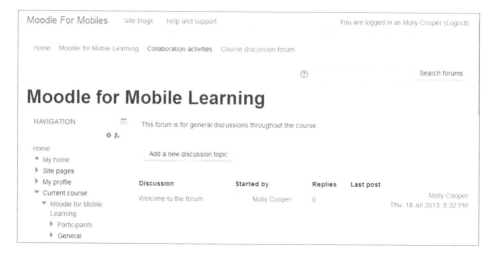

Learner view of group discussion

Perform the following steps as a learner:

1. Navigate to the discussion activity from your course page. Click on a discussion item to view it.

2. The discussion item view has a drop-down list for viewing the forum in different modes (for example, oldest or newest first). Click on **Reply**.

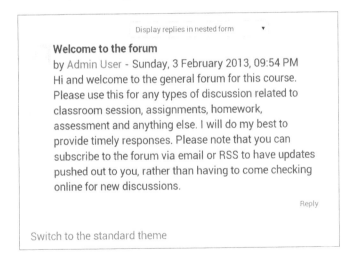

3. Type your reply, and then click on **Post to forum**.

4. The forum view now contains the post that you just added.

Communicating through social networks

There will be a time in a course where students need to approach tutors for advice and support regarding the subject matter of the course or any technical or administrative queries they may have. It is important that there are clear and appropriate channels for such support.

While real-time chat rooms can be used on a weekly basis as a valuable place for support, a more informal and ad-hoc support channel is also needed. Most students are already connecting on social networks such as Facebook, Twitter, and Google+. It makes sense to "go to where the fish are" and open up the channel of communication with them on those networks. Many social networks produce widgets that you can add to your own site.

> One method to facilitate informal support is to use the **Online Users** block, which can be added to a course page and shows which course participants are online within the last five minutes, and from where you can click an icon next to users' names in order to send them a message via the Moodle messaging feature.

Adding a Google+ contact badge

To add a Google+ contact badge to a course topic summary, perform the following steps:

1. Go to `https://developers.google.com/+/web/badge/` and select the badge that you would like to display on your Moodle page.

2. Copy the code snippet, and then go to your Moodle page in a new browser window.

3. Click on **Turn editing on**.

4. Edit a label or topic summary, and then click on the HTML icon to toggle into HTML mode.

5. Paste the code snippet, and then click on **Update**.

6. Add some text if you wish, and then click on **Save changes**.

Welcome to the Mobile learning in HE/FE page. Here you will find resources related to this chapter of the book and some sample activities.

I encourage you to communicate with me on Google+. Add me to your circles and feel free to get in touch to talk about Moodle for mobile learning or suggest resources and case studies that you think should be added to this page.

Mark Aberdour on   Add to circles

Twitter hashtag feeds

Twitter is the social networking site that allows user to broadcast short, 140-character messages to all Twitter users. Hashtags such as #Moodle or #OpenSource are commonly used to tag posts and act as a search filter so that users can view all #Moodle posts, for example. Courses will often have a unique hashtag so that students can find each other's tweets easily.

Given the ease with which students can tweet on the move and from any location, this type of activity is very well suited to mobile learning. It can be useful to have a Twitter hashtag feed displaying in a block on your course page. You can then set up a hash tag for your course, and have this display on the course page. Real world examples of this type of activity include students tweeting to a Twitter stream what they enjoyed most about a particular lesson, a class connecting with authors over Twitter, and pulling the Twitter hashtag stream into Moodle.

Setting up a Twitter hashtag feed

To setup a hashtag feed perform the following steps:

1. In your browser, go to `https://twitter.com/settings/widgets/`.
2. In the **Widgets** menu, click on **Create new**.
3. Under **Choose a timeline source**, select **Search**.
4. In the search box, type your hashtag name, for example, #moodle.
5. Click on **Create widget**.

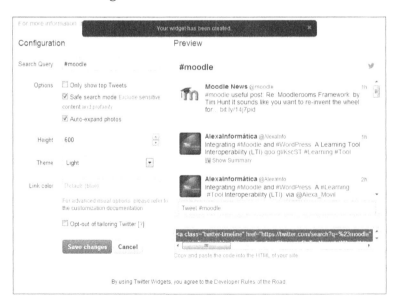

6. In Moodle, enter your course page, and click on **Turn editing on**.

7. Find the block called **ADD A BLOCK,** which should be at the bottom of the left column, and select **HTML** from the drop-down list.

8. This will create a new, empty HTML block. Click on the configuration icon within this new block.

9. This will launch a new page titled **Configuring a (new HTML block) block**. In the **Content** section, click on the small button labeled **HTML**.

10. This will launch the **HTML source editor**. Go back to your Twitter Widget page and select the highlighted text just above the instruction: **Copy and paste the code into the HTML source editor**. Do not worry about the content of the code snippet; it contains a lot of JavaScript that you do not need to understand—this is really just an exercise in copy and paste!

11. Click on **Update**, and then on the Moodle page click on **Save changes**.

12. The block will now be displayed on the bottom-left of your Moodle page. The first time it displays it may take a few seconds to retrieve the tweets from Twitter. You can use the arrow icon on the top of the block to move it to any location in the left or right columns.

Learner view of a Twitter hashtag feed

The desktop view shows the three-column layout:

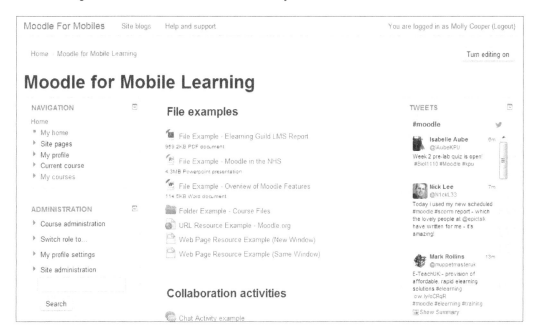

Other Twitter widgets

More Twitter code snippets can be found at:

```
https://twitter.com/settings/widgets/.
```

These allow you to include items such as the **Follow** button, to enable users to quickly follow you on Twitter, and the **Tweet** button, which will allow an instant tweet with a link to the page. This latter option is great to allow students to share pages or resources with their network.

Managing the backchannel

A backchannel is the social media presence that forms around a real-world event. If you attend technology conferences, you may sometimes see a hashtag promoting the event such as #mootie13 which was the hashtag for the Ireland Moodlemoot 2013. The community that forms during the event around this hashtag is known as the **backchannel**. These do not have to be unique to conferences though, and backchannels can form around short, one hour classroom events or web conferences. The backchannel provides an excellent opportunity to students to discuss the event while it is happening and engage in some networking.

Using Twitter backchannels

Role: Tutor	**Time**: 15 minutes and above	**Device**: Smartphone or Tablet

All you need to do here is communicate a hashtag to your students that is identifiable with your lecture. Put the hashtag in the footer of each slide if you are using a slide deck, or stick it on the wall somewhere visible. This will enable them to set up a hashtag search on their mobiles and watch the Twitter feed for that come in.

A hashtag feed can be collected afterwards and posted to your Moodle course page. Tools come and go but currently Tweetarchivist.com offers a good free service that will collect the tweets together in one place, allow you to download a PDF or XLS file, and provide a number of good analytics about top tweeters and top words.

Using Moodle chat backchannels

Role: Tutor	**Time**: 15 minutes and above	**Device**: Smartphone or Tablet

The alternative is to run a chat room directly in Moodle, which is useful as the chat logs can be automatically captured. To add a new Chat activity, perform the following steps:

1. On your course page, click on **Turn editing on**, and then in one of your topic areas select **Add an activity or resource,** and click on **Chat**.

2. On the **Adding a new Chat** page, under the **Chat sessions** subheading, fill in the following fields as appropriate:

    ◦ **Next chat time**: If you change this to the time of lecture, the chat area will not open until this time

    ◦ **Repeat/publish session times**: You can use this to schedule repeating sessions

    ◦ **Save past sessions**: Here, there are a number of options but the best one would be to **Never delete messages**

    ◦ **Everyone can view past sessions:** If you select **Yes** then all course users can see the chat logs, which is normally what you would want

3. Click on **Save and return to course**.

4. For a student, there are two options when entering a chat room — standard or accessible interface. Right now the chat interface is only really usable on mobile devices when using the accessible interface.

Using Moodle messaging

Moodle has a built-in messaging system that allows conversations between users and notifications about system events, such as new forum posts or assignment submissions. This is useful for mobile learning because the user has a high level of control over their personal messaging settings and can configure notifications about all sorts of system events to be sent to their personal e-mail accounts when they are on the move.

Messages can be accessed from several places:

• Directly from the **Messages** block, if it is enabled. This block will also show whether you have new messages

• From the **People** block, by clicking on **Participants**, then selecting one or more users, and clicking on **Send a message**

• Through the **Navigation** block, by clicking on **My profile** | **Messages**

• Via a link on the site header bar if you enable it (see the *Adding a messaging link in the site header* section)

Users can edit their messaging settings by navigating **ADMINISTRATION** | **My profile settings** | **Messaging**. The resulting page allows them to configure whether to receive e-mail or pop-up notifications for a range of different system events, such as assignment notifications, essay grading notifications, and personal messages. For each system event, the user can select whether to receive a pop-up notification or an e-mail when they are either offline or online.

Note that "offline" does not mean logged out; it means that the user has been inactive for at least five minutes or whatever time frame is configured by navigating **ADMINISTRATION | Site administration | Plugins | Blocks | Online users**.

Sending a message via the Moodle Mobile app

To send a message to a user by using the Moodle Mobile app, perform the following steps:

1. Log in to the app and click on your course title to expand the menu to display the contents and participants. Click on **Participants,** as shown in the following left-side screenshot. The **Participants** page opens as shown in the following right-side screenshot; select the name of the user you want to message.

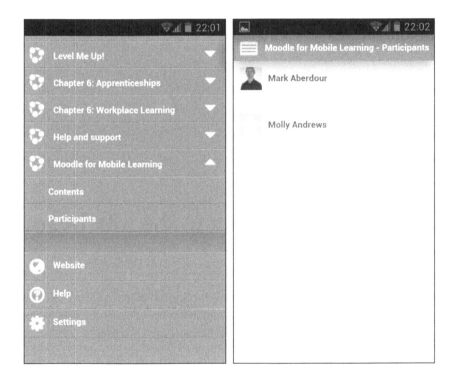

2. On the User page (shown in the following left-side screenshot), there are a number of buttons available to choose from. Select **Send a message** from the list of options. This opens the **Send a message** window (shown in the right-hand screenshot) where you can write your message. Click on the **Send a message** button to complete the task.

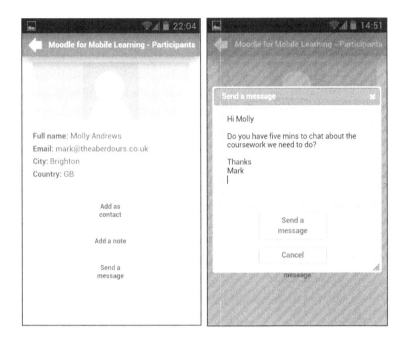

Adding a messaging link to the site header

Role: Admin	Time: 15 minutes and above	Device: Desktop

Adding a messaging link to the site header will give a handy tip to mobile users, to allow them to quickly access the messaging function without having to scroll through the **NAVIGATION** block, or add the **People** or **Messages** blocks, which add additional clutter to a small mobile device screen. To add a messaging link, perform the following steps:

1. Navigate to **ADMINISTRATION** | **Site administration** | **Appearance** | **Theme** | **Theme settings**.

2. Scroll down to the field **Custom menu items**. You can add menu items into the empty text box. Each line consists of the menu text, a link URL and a tool-tip title, separated by pipe characters.

3. To add a messages link you can add the text `http://www.moodleformobiles.com/ message/index.php|Messages` replacing `www.moodleformobiles.com` with your own site's homepage URL.

This will display the link on the header bar throughout the site, and will be very easily accessible from a mobile device when using the Bootstrap theme, for example:

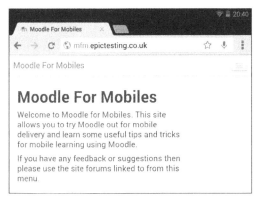

Sending SMS notifications

There are several Moodle plugins relating to SMS messaging, most notably the **moodletxt** plugin, which allows teachers and administrators to send personalized SMS text messages to their students from within Moodle. There is also an extension plugin called **moodletxt+,** which will send automatic SMS messages on system events such as site and course notifications.

The moodletxt plugin will need to be installed by your site administrator. The plugin can be downloaded from the Moodle plugins database at `moodle.org/plugins`. The service requires an account with Blackboard connecttxt, and trial accounts can be provided on request.

The company behind moodletxt was called txttools and they have been acquired by Blackboard and became their Blackboard **Connecttxt** product; however, the Moodle plugins remain supported and should do so for the foreseeable future, given Blackboard's acquisition of two major Moodle partner companies: Moodlerooms and Netspot.

Setting up a real-time chat session

Role: Tutor	**Time**: 10 minutes	**Device**: Desktop

Real-time chat is an important component of distance learning because it reclaims some of the spontaneity and student collaboration that occurs with face to face courses but which can be easily lost with distance learning. Real-time chat can be used in a number of scenarios:

- Immediately after specific events such as online lectures
- Left open at all times for anyone to chat with whomever happens to be online
- Weekly organized sessions
- Q&A sessions with an invited speaker

Chat logs, particularly regarding specific chat "events" can be captured and published for the benefit of students at a later date.

To set up an organized chat session, perform the following steps:

1. Click on the **Turn editing on** button, select **Add an activity or resource**, choose **Chat** from the drop-down menu, and then click on **Add**.

2. On the **Adding a new Chat** page, under the **Chat sessions** subheading, fill in the following fields as appropriate:

   ° **Next chat time:** If you change this to the time of lecture, the chat area will not open until this time

   ° **Repeat / publish session times**: Use this to schedule repeating sessions

   ° **Save past sessions**: Here there are a number of options, but the best one would be to **Never delete messages**

   ° **Everyone can view past sessions**: If you select **Yes** then all course users can see the chat logs, which is normally what you would want

3. Click on **Save and return to course** or **Save and display**, as required.

 For large online distance-learning courses it would be a good idea, when using weekly chat sessions, to either move the sessions between time zones to give students in different parts of world opportunity to engage, during more reasonable hours. Alternatively, you could run a small number of weekly sessions in three or four time zones, to give better global coverage.

Participating in a chat session

Role: Student	**Time**: 15 minutes and above	**Device**: Smartphone or Tablet

To participate in an organized chat session, a user will perform the following steps:

1. Click on the title of the chat session.

 Weekly chat session

Every week at this time we hold a one hour chat session in order that students and tutors can engage online. *Mobile device users please note that you should select the 'Accessible' option when entering the session in order to view it properly.*

2. At this point the user has two options. Mobile device users should select the **Use more accessible interface** option, as the standard Moodle chat is not suited to small-screened mobile devices—even seven inch tablets.

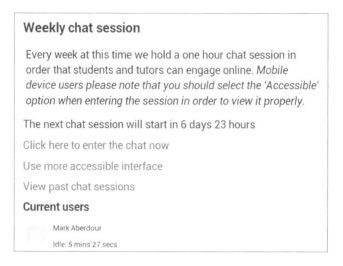

3. The accessible chat interface will allow users to post and view messages, and to see who is online. It is the same functionality as the standard interface, but laid out more appropriately for smaller screens.

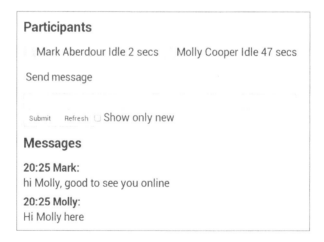

Setting up a virtual classroom plugin

| **Role**: Admin | **Time**: 15 minutes and above | **Device**: Desktop |

Virtual classrooms—also commonly known as webinars or web conferencing—introduce an important element of synchronous learning into online courses, which can lead to higher engagement and enhanced interaction among students.

 On distance-learning courses, virtual classroom sessions need to be carefully scheduled in order not to conflict with the schedule flexibility that appeals to many distance learning students.

Typically, a virtual classroom session will consist of a presenter and multiple attendees, in which the presenter uses webcam video and a slide-show or screen sharing to deliver a presentation, while attendees can interact with each other using a chat panel, and can contribute to the presentation by using an electronic whiteboard, or can be temporarily handed the presenter role to share their own screens or webcam.

There are a number of key players in the virtual classroom market, many of which have plugins for Moodle. These include commercial tools such as Blackboard Collaborate, Adobe Connect Pro, and Cisco WebEx, and open source tools such as Big Blue Button.

 The commercial tools are mostly hosted offerings and come at an annual subscription cost, although some can be downloaded and installed on your own server. But beware; these are server-hungry applications that consume a great deal of bandwidth. Think very carefully and talk to your IT team before installing one on your own servers. The open source tools are also available as hosted offerings at lower cost, and have the downloadable option too, in which case the same risks apply.

We will use Adobe Connect Pro (ACP) as an example here, which itself is a mobile-friendly web conferencing tool, using the open source Webinar plugin which is available on the Moodle plugins database at `moodle.org/plugins/`. For the following steps, we will assume that the plugin is already downloaded and installed:

1. Navigate to **ADMINISTRATION** | **Site administration** | **Plugins** | **Activity modules** | **Webinar**.

2. There are just three fields to fill in here:

   ° **Site XML API URL**: This will be your ACP login URL followed by `/api/xml`

   ° **Administrator email**: This will be the e-mail address of the ACP account administrator

   ° **Administrator password**: This will have been chosen on ACP account signup or changed since

3. Once the settings have been specified, click on **Save changes**.

Setting up a virtual classroom session

Role: Tutor	**Time**: 10 minutes	**Device**: Desktop or Tablet

Using the Webinar plugin as described in the previous section, you will need to add a Webinar activity into your course page. Go to the course you wish to use and perform the following steps:

1. Click on **Add an activity or resource** and select **Webinar**.

2. In the **Add a new Webinar** screen, there are three fields to complete:

   ° **Name** (the required field)

   ° **Description**

   ° **Agenda**

3. Once completed, click on **Save and display**.

4. You will now be on the **Activity screen,** and can start adding sessions. Click on **Add a new session** to add your first one.

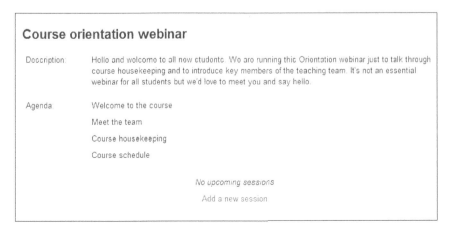

5. You will now be in the **Adding a new session** screen. Here you can update following four fields:

    ○   **Host**: This will list any user enrolled in the course as Administrator, Teacher or Non-Editing Teacher. Some Adobe Connect accounts only allow a single host, in which case the selected user in this field *must* be the Adobe Connect account holder and be registered in Moodle with the same e-mail address.

    ○   **Capacity**: This is is the maximum amount of users you want to be able to attend the webinar.

    ○   **Start date/time**: The date and time at which the webinar starts.

    ○   **Finish date/time**: The date and time at which the webinar ends.

6. Click on **Save changes** to save the session and return to the Webinar activity screen. You will now see the webinar details:

7. Students can now enroll themselves onto the webinar.

8. As the teacher, you can now open the session at the allotted time by clicking on **Join session as host**. This will initiate the webinar session, after which students will also be able to join the live webinar.

9. Clicking on **Join session as host** launches the ACP window, at which point the virtual classroom session will be live. Your students will be shown in the **Attendees** window. Consult your ACP help guide on using the tool itself.

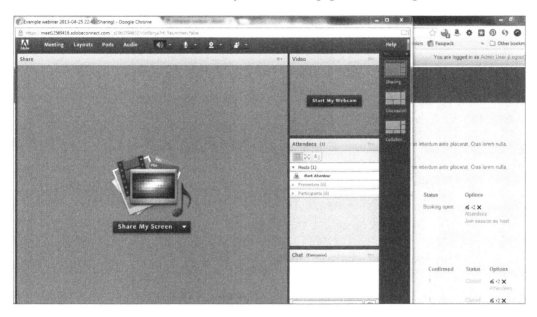

Joining a web conference

Role: Student	Time: 5 minutes	Device: Smartphone or Tablet

Students will be able to self-enroll on web conference sessions by performing the following steps:

1. Click on the activity name and link on your Moodle course page.

2. On the webinar activity screen, select the session you wish to register for, and click on **Register**.

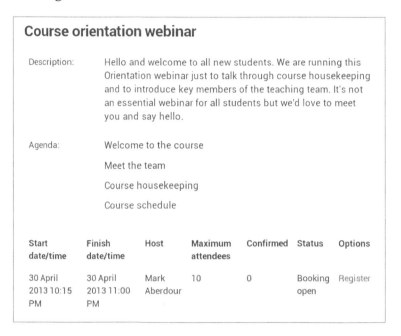

3. On the next screen, click on the **Sign-up** button to confirm your registration.

4. You will then see a confirmation message. Click on the **Continue** link.

Registration successful

You have successfully registered on Course orientation webinar.
(Continue)

5. The webinar activity screen is now updated. You can click on **Cancel booking** if you wish to cancel this booking. Once the session has started, you can click on **Join session** to join the webinar.

Start date/time	Finish date/time	Host	Maximum attendees	Confirmed	Status	Options
30 April 2013 10:15 PM	30 April 2013 11:00 PM	Mark Aberdour	10	1	Wait-listed	Cancel booking Join session

6. At this point, you may be prompted to install the Adobe Connect Pro mobile app if you have not yet done so. You will then join the session in the Adobe Connect app, which on a tablet will look like the following screenshot:

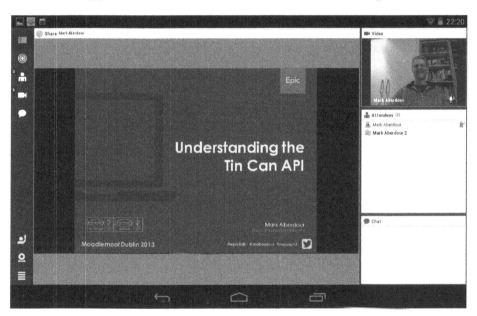

Summary

In this chapter, we looked at the wide range of communication tools in Moodle and how these can be used in a mobile learning context. First we looked at group discussion features, then social network integration, messaging and SMS, and finally at virtual classroom activities.

Appendix

You can read more about *Mobile Learning* from *Research Library* of *The eLearning Guild* at `http://www.elearningguild.com/research/archives/index.cfm?id=117&action=viewonly`.

You can get the book *The Mobile Academy: mLearning for Higher Education* at `http://www.amazon.com/Mobile-Academy-mLearning-Education-JOSSEY-BASS/dp/1118072650`.

You can download the app *Adult Drug Calculations* (Android Apps on Google Play) from `https://play.google.com/store/apps/details?id=air.adc&feature=more_from_developer`.

You can read more about *Our Mobile Planet* from *Think with Google* at `http://www.thinkwithgoogle.com/mobileplanet/en/`.

You can read about *Percentage of Individuals using the Internet Metadata for...* (ITU) at `http://www.itu.int/ITU-D/ict/statistics/material/excel/Individuals%20using%20the%20Internet2000-2011_Oct.xls`.

You can read more about *Trends in Digital Device and Internet Usage 2012* from *Think with Google* at `http://www.thinkwithgoogle.com/insights/library/studies/trends-in-digital-device-and-internet-usage-2012/`.

You can refer to *Cell Internet Use 2012* from *Pew Internet & American Life Project* at `http://pewinternet.org/Reports/2012/Cell-Internet-Use-2012/Main-Findings/Cell-Internet-Use.aspx`.

You can refer to *How Cellphones Shape the Lives of College Students [INFOGRAPHIC]* from *Mashable* at `http://mashable.com/2011/10/31/cellphones-college-students/`.

You can refer about *Moodle Statistics* at `https://moodle.org/stats/`.

You can refer to *The New Multi-Screen World* from *Think with Google* at `http://www.thinkwithgoogle.com/insights/featured/new-multi-screen-world-insight/`.

You can refer to *The 12 Most Popular Ways College Students Use Smartphones* at `http://edudemic.com/2012/12/the-12-most-popular-ways-college-students-use-smartphones/`.

You can refer to *Connecting in the 21st Century: Parents and Administrators Speak Up about Effective School to Home Communications* from *Project Tomorrow* at `http://www.tomorrow.org/speakup/Connecting21st_2012.html`.

You can refer to *What do High School students want from mobile tech? [Infographic]* from *ZDNet* at `http://www.zdnet.com/blog/igeneration/what-do-high-school-students-want-from-mobile-tech-infographic/15843`.

You can refer to *Consumerization of IT* from *avanade* at `http://www.avanade.com/en-us/approach/research/Pages/consumerization-of-it.aspx`.

You can read about *The Latest Infographics: Mobile Business Statistics For 2012* from *Forbes* at `http://www.forbes.com/sites/markfidelman/2012/05/02/the-latest-infographics-mobile-business-statistics-for-2012/`.

Index

A

Adobe Connect Pro (ACP) 202
AICC packages 62
App library
  learner view 58
  setting up 56-58
assignment
  files, adding 119-121
  setting up, for file submission 110-112
  used, for grading reflective log 137, 138
  used, for reviewing reflective log 137, 138
  used, for setting up reflective log 131-133
  used, for submitting reflective log 134-136
assignment briefing document
  creating, for offline viewing 110
audio 87
audio add-ons 91
audio assignments
  examples 109
audio feedback
  providing 92-97
audio instruction
  providing 91, 92

B

backchannel
  about 192
  managing 192
Big Blue Button 201
Blackboard Collaborate 201
Blackboard Connecttxt product 198
Blogs link
  adding, in site header 146, 147

Book module
  about 43
  used, for adding help and support guides
    43-46
Bootstrap theme
  about 25, 26
  downloading 32-34
  installing 32-34
  setting up 36
BYOD (Bring Your Own Device)
  about 18
  implementations 16

C

capabilities, mobile devices 8, 9
case studies, mobile learning strategy
  about 19
  Open University 23, 24
  University of Sussex 20-22
chat session
  participating in 199, 200
  setting up 198, 199
Cisco WebEx 201
Clean theme
  about 26, 27
  exploring 29-31
  setting up 27, 28
cohorts
  setting up 70-74
  used, for delivering performance-support
    resources 69-74
communicating
  through social networks 186
course blog post
  submitting 145

course blogs
  about 143
  Moodle, setting up for 143, 145
courses
  QR codes, using in 59, 60
course topic summary
  Google+ contact badge, adding 187

D

Database assignment
  setting up 122-125
  submitting 126-130
Droodle 42

E

Echo360 98
ePortfolio tool 131

F

Facebook 187
feature phone 9
file assignment
  submitting 112-115
  submitting, Moodle Mobile app used 118,
    119
file downloads
  learner view 54, 55
  setting up 51-54
files
  adding, in assignments 119-121
file submission
  assignment, setting up for 110-112
file types 56
flipped classroom approach 99
formative assessment
  building, quiz activity used 154-158
  question bank, building 158-160
  quiz, accessing 162-166
  quiz, building 160-162
  quiz, creating for 153
  quiz, setting up 154-158
  skills gap analysis, performing 166-172
forums 139

G

Glossary
  using, for best practice resource collection
    80
  using, for staff induction 74-79
Google 11
Google+ 187
Google+ contact badge
  adding, in course topic summary 187
grades
  checking 178
group discussion forum
  learner view 185, 186
  setting up 182-184

H

hashtags 188
header bar
  link, adding to help and support 47, 48
help and support
  link, adding to 48

I

iActive 42
IMS Content Package 63
individual forums
  used, for reviewing reflective log 142, 143
  used, for setting up reflective log 139, 140
  used, for submitting reflective log 140, 141
Information Security Awareness Learning
    Suite. *See* Infosec
information security awareness training
  about 68
  multidevice SCORM resource, using for 68,
    69
Infosec 68

J

journals 131

L

learner view, App library 58
learner view, file downloads 54, 55

learner view, group discussion forum 185, 186
learner view, podcast 90
learner view, Twitter hashtag feed 191
Learning Tools Interoperability (LTI) 98
lecture-cast products 97
Lecturecasts
  delivering, to mobiles 97-99
Lesson activity
  creating, steps 100-106
levels
  used, for engaging learners 81-86
link
  adding, to help and support 47, 48

M

Mahara 131
Massive Online Open Courses (MOOCs) 18
mDroid 42
media capture 91
message
  sending, in Moodle Mobile app 195, 196
messaging link
  adding, in site header 196, 197
mobile devices
  capabilities 8, 9
mobile learning
  about 7, 8
  in academic research 17
  learners 11, 12
  users 10, 11
mobile learning strategy
  about 10
  case studies 19
mobiles
  Lecturecasts, delivering to 97-99
mobile usage
  in apprenticeships 17
  in distance learning 18, 19
  in further and higher education 14-17
  in organization 13
  in school 13
  in workplace 18
Moodle
  multidevice SCORM resource, adding into 62-67

setting up, for course blogs 143, 145
Moodle chat backchannels
  using 193, 194
MoodleEZ (MoodleEasy) 42
Moodle for Android 42
Moodle messaging
  message, sending in Moodle Mobile app 196
  messaging link, adding in site header 197
  SMS notifications, sending 197, 198
  using 194
Moodle Mobile app
  about 26, 37
  exploring 39-41
  functions 37
  message, sending in 195, 196
  setting up 38
  used, for submitting assignment 116-119
  working 39
Moodlerooms 198
moodletxt+ 197
moodletxt plugin 197
mTouch 41
multidevice SCORM resource
  adding, into Moodle 62-67
  building 61
  using, for information security awareness training 68, 69
MyMobile theme 26

N

Netspot 198
Nintendo DS 13

O

offline viewing
  assignment briefing document, creating for 110
Onefile 131
online audio recording 91
online communication tools 181
Open University (OU) case study 23, 24

P

performance-support resources
  delivering, cohorts used 69-74
photo assignments
  examples 110
PlayStation 13
podcast
  learner view 90
  setting up 88, 90
podcasting
  advantages 87
  disadvantages 88
portfolio
  work, exporting to 149-151
portfolio export
  enabling 148
practice resource collection
  Glossary, using for 80

Q

QR codes
  about 59
  using, in courses 59, 60
question bank
  building, for formative assessment 158-160
quiz
  creating, for formative assessment 153
  creating, for summative assessment 173
quiz activity
  used, for building formative assessment 154-158
  used, for building summative assessment 174, 175

R

real-time chat 198
record audio 91
reflective log
  about 131
  grading, Assignment used 137, 138
  reviewing, Assignment used 137, 138
  reviewing, individual forums used 142, 143
  setting up, Assignment used 131-133

setting up, individual forums used 139, 140
submitting, Assignment used 134-136
submitting, individual forums used 140, 141

S

SCORM 61, 63
SCORM 1.2 62
SCORM activity
  adding, into Moodle 63-67
Sharable Content Object Reference Model.
  See **SCORM**
site header
  Blogs link, adding 146, 147
  messaging link, adding 196, 197
skills gap analysis
  about 166
  performing 166-172
smartphones 9
SMS notifications
  sending 197
social networks
  communicating through 186
staff induction
  Glossary, using for 74-79
Study Direct 20
summative assessment
  about 173
  building, Quiz activity used 174, 175
  quiz, accessing 175-178
  quiz, creating for 173
  quiz, setting up 174

T

tablets 9
themes 25
third-party Moodle apps
  Droodle 42
  iActive 42
  mDroid 42
  MoodleEZ (MoodleEasy) 42
  Moodle for Android 42
  mTouch 41
  umm (Unofficial Moodle Mobile) 42

Tweetarchivist.com 192
Twitter 187, 188
Twitter backchannels
  using 192
Twitter hashtag feed
  learner view 191
  setting up 188-190
Twitter widgets 191
txttools 198

U

umm (Unofficial Moodle Mobile) 27, 42
University of Sussex case study 20-22

V

video assignments
  examples 109
video lesson
  creating 99

virtual classroom plugin
  setting up 201, 202
virtual classroom session
  setting up 202-205
virtual learning environment (VLE) 15

W

web conference
  joining 205, 206
webinars 201
work
  exporting, to portfolio 149-151

Y

YouTube submission 91

Thank you for buying
Moodle for Mobile Learning

About Packt Publishing

Packt, pronounced 'packed', published its first book "*Mastering phpMyAdmin for Effective MySQL Management*" in April 2004 and subsequently continued to specialize in publishing highly focused books on specific technologies and solutions.

Our books and publications share the experiences of your fellow IT professionals in adapting and customizing today's systems, applications, and frameworks. Our solution based books give you the knowledge and power to customize the software and technologies you're using to get the job done. Packt books are more specific and less general than the IT books you have seen in the past. Our unique business model allows us to bring you more focused information, giving you more of what you need to know, and less of what you don't.

Packt is a modern, yet unique publishing company, which focuses on producing quality, cutting-edge books for communities of developers, administrators, and newbies alike. For more information, please visit our website: www.packtpub.com.

About Packt Open Source

In 2010, Packt launched two new brands, Packt Open Source and Packt Enterprise, in order to continue its focus on specialization. This book is part of the Packt Open Source brand, home to books published on software built around Open Source licences, and offering information to anybody from advanced developers to budding web designers. The Open Source brand also runs Packt's Open Source Royalty Scheme, by which Packt gives a royalty to each Open Source project about whose software a book is sold.

Writing for Packt

We welcome all inquiries from people who are interested in authoring. Book proposals should be sent to author@packtpub.com. If your book idea is still at an early stage and you would like to discuss it first before writing a formal book proposal, contact us; one of our commissioning editors will get in touch with you.

We're not just looking for published authors; if you have strong technical skills but no writing experience, our experienced editors can help you develop a writing career, or simply get some additional reward for your expertise.

Moodle 2 for Teaching 7-14 Year Olds Beginner's Guide

ISBN: 978-1-849518-32-1   Paperback: 258 pages

Effective e-learning for younger students, using Moodle as your classroom assistant

1. Ideal for teachers new to Moodle: easy to follow and abundantly illustrated with screenshots of the solutions you'll build

2. Go paperless! Put your lessons online and grade them anywhere, anytime

3. Engage and motivate your students with games, quizzes, movies, blogs, and podcasts the whole class can participate in

Blackboard Learn Administration

ISBN: 978-1-849693-06-6   Paperback: 326 pages

Discover how to administrate your Blackboard Leearn platform through step-by-step tutorials

1. Learn both the simple and the complex skills to become an expert Blackboard Learn admin

2. Optimize the security and performance of Blackboard Learn and create a disaster recovery plan

3. Gain insight from an experienced Blackboard administrator using a hands-on approach

Please check **www.PacktPub.com** for information on our titles

Desire2Learn for Higher Education Cookbook

ISBN: 978-1-849693-44-8   Paperback: 206 pages

Gain expert knowledge of the tools within Desire2Learn, maximize your productivity, and create online learning experiences with these easy-to-follow recipes

Desire2Learn for Higher Education Cookbook

Gain expert knowledge of the tools within the Desire2Learn Learning Environment, maximize your productivity, and create online learning experiences with these easy-to-follow recipes

Brandon Ballentine

1. Customize the look and feel of your online course, integrate graphics and video, and become more productive using the learning environment's built-in assessment and collaboration tools

2. Recipes address real world challenges in clear and concise step-by-step instructions, which help you work your way through technical tasks with ease

3. Detailed instructions with screenshots to guide you through each task

---

Learning Adobe Connect 9

ISBN: 978-1-849694-16-2   Paperback: 178 pages

Successfully create and host web meetings, virtual classes, and webinars with Adobe Connect

Learning Adobe Connect 9

Successfully create and host web meetings, virtual classes, and webinars with Adobe Connect

Miloš Radovanović   Miloš Vučetić

1. Master all the important features of Adobe Connect

2. Utilize Adobe Connect for your mission critical web conferencing needs, independent of the type of user devices

3. A practical guide to effectively use Adobe Connect for small team collaboration or large-scale meetings, presentations, training, and online events

Please check **www.PacktPub.com** for information on our titles

Lightning Source UK Ltd.
Milton Keynes UK
UKOW06f2002280115

245300UK00004B/257/P